A PORTRAIT OF
GOD

A PORTRAIT OF GOD

STEPHEN CHARNOCK'S
DISCOURSES UPON THE EXISTENCE
AND ATTRIBUTES OF GOD

SUMMARIZED FOR THE 21ST CENTURY

DANIEL CHAMBERLIN

FREE GRACE PRESS

A Portrait of God: Stephen Charnock's Discourses upon the Existence and Attributes of God, Summarized for the 21st Century

Copyright © 2022 Daniel Chamberlin

Published by
Free Grace Press
3900 Dave Ward Dr., Ste. 1900
Conway, AR 72034
(501) 214-9663
email: support@freegracepress.com
website: www.freegracepress.com

Printed in the United States of America

Cover Design by Scott Schaller
scottschallerdesigns.com

Scripture quotations are from the King James Bible (KJV). Public domain.

ISBN: 978-1-952599-52-1

For additional Reformed Baptist titles, please email us
for a free list or see our website at the above address.

CONTENTS

Foreword

This book is a treasure. For the thoughtful Christian, it expounds in an accessible manner the nature of the living God. Consider reading a couple of pages a day during your daily devotions. The benefit to your spiritual life will be beyond measure as your conception of God is enlarged and corrected.

For the pastor, this work is a gold mine. It will feed your soul, suggest endless sermons, and provide a main source for any series on the attributes of God.

Pastor Daniel Chamberlin has done his work well. Only God knows the labor that has gone into such a skillful effort to make Charnock available to our busy age. Your benefit will be Pastor Chamberlin's reward.

So great is the value of Charnock, his full-length study is still in print. But because of its size, it is seldom read. Should you have the money and the space, buy the original. It will look nice on your shelf. But I say in all sincerity, keep this little volume on your desk!

A Christian friend,

Ron Crisp

April 2011

PREFACE

The knowledge of God is indispensable to all other knowledge. The folly that abounds today in religion, not to mention in the world, is symptomatic of an underlying ignorance of God. Superficiality is the order of the day. But previous generations thought and wrote more profoundly about God. Perhaps the greatest uninspired author on this vital subject was Stephen Charnock (1628–1680), who wrote *Discourses Upon the Existence and Attributes of God*. This honored treatise is especially valuable for its pastoral and practical application. In the pages before you is my summary of that treatise. I have attempted to be as transparent as possible and let Mr. Charnock speak.

Why summarize Charnock? Because many in these regrettably rushed times will never find time to read the original, which extends to more than 1,100 pages. Furthermore, I hope this summary will enable translators to bring the riches of the treatise to languages and nations that otherwise would never get to enjoy them.

My thanks go to my family for their patience while I was absorbed in this demanding but happy task. (My wife claims she was married to Charnock for several years!) Likewise, thanks to my church for allowing me to give myself to this project. Thanks to Brother Ron Crisp for his encouragement, insisting that my manuscript be raised from its seven-year dormancy. Finally, thanks to Brother Ben Gardner for his proofreading and suggestions.

I cannot estimate the personal blessing I have received by studying and preaching this material as well as preparing it for publication. I find myself referring to these precious truths frequently in my own mind. I pray that you might find it a blessing as well.

Daniel Chamberlin

April 2011

1

THE EXISTENCE OF GOD

In Psalm 14:1 we read, "The fool hath said in his heart, There is no God." The apostle Paul refers to this same psalm in Romans 3 to prove that every person in the whole world is corrupt in sin. In our hearts, every one of us is in some sense an atheist.

The Hebrew term translated *God* in Psalm 14:1 is not *Jehovah*, which speaks of His existence. Rather, it is *Elohia*, which speaks of His being the Judge. This is what natural man finds offensive—that God should stand over him and call him to account for his sin. Many people are willing to acknowledge a deity as long as it is not the *Elohia* of Scripture. But true religion requires we believe not only that God exists but also that He exists with the character Scripture reveals. In the words of Hebrews 11:6, we must believe that God is and that He is a rewarder of those who diligently seek Him.

There are three kinds of atheism. First, absolute atheism denies altogether that there is a God. Second, providential atheism confines God to heaven and keeps Him from earth. Deism falls into this category. Third, natural atheism denies the nature and perfections attributed to God in the Scripture. This kind of atheism is the most common and the most subtle. How many church members confess there is a God but deny Him the fullness of character described in His Word!

Every atheist is a great fool. He goes against all reason and ultimately denies everything. His conscience tells him there is a God, but he insists on suppressing and denying this knowledge (Rom.

1:18). He is left with nothing. To make a man complete, religion is as necessary as reason.

To show how foolish atheism is, let us consider some arguments for the existence of God.

The Universal Prevalence of Religion Is Evidence for the Existence of God

History shows us man's religious orientation. All societies were and are permeated with religion of some kind. To deny the existence of God is to deny what all men have always known. It is sheer folly to deny what every man's conscience tells him.

The fact that many societies believed in a multiplicity of gods does not weaken this argument. It simply confirms the religious nature of man. Man was originally made a worshiper. In the fall, his concept of God was marred, yet he continues a worshiper, albeit of false gods.

Of all the great disputes in human history, the existence of God was not one of them. Many matters of religion were hotly disputed, but everyone agreed there is a God. The few exceptions to this rule do not negate the principle. Just because some people are physically blind, we do not conclude that eyesight is not natural to mankind! Nor do the few absolute atheists prove that man is not a natural worshiper.

Men would have gotten rid of this God-consciousness if they could, but it remains constant. Acknowledging a deity is essential to our very being. Even Satan never tried to root out this principle in the original temptation. Rather, when tempting Eve, he distorted the word and character of God.

Religion is innate to man. The law of God is written in our hearts, and our conscience bears a witness to it (Rom. 2:15). The religious nature of man is not received by mere tradition. All traditions are lost over the passing of time, but this God-consciousness remains in everyone.

Some people argue that social engineers invented religion to keep the people "in line" and under their subjection. But those who teach such an idea cannot answer the following questions: Who were these engineers of society? How did they all come to agree? How could they have accomplished their purpose so universally in every age? How have they managed to keep this manipulation a secret?

Some say that fear first introduced religion. "Feelings of guilt made man come up with the idea of God," they say. They are actually thinking backward. It is the knowledge of God that brings fear and guilt to sinful man.

The Universe Is Evidence for the Existence of God

Romans 1:19–20 affirms this truth: "Because that which may be known of God is manifest in them; for God hath showed it unto them. For the invisible things of him from the creation of the world are clearly seen, being understood by the things that are made, even his eternal power and Godhead; so that they are without excuse."

All Things Point to God in Their Origin and Production

Every effect must have a cause. For example, every building has its architect and builder. To deny this truth is indeed to be *without excuse*! Everything came from somewhere. Ultimately, we are left with only two possibilities: either God is eternal or matter is eternal. Since it is inconceivable that intelligent personality should spring from inanimate matter, the only rational position is to say that matter sprang from an intelligent person—namely, God—who made all things out of nothing.

Even time must have an origin. Time is motion, and all motion has a beginning. There is no perpetual motion—not even in time.

Both time and man himself must have an origin. Reason dictates to us that there must be a beginning, at which point a cause set the effect in motion. The cause must be of a different kind than the effect, superior to it in every way. Otherwise, we run into inconceivable contradictions. There must be one infinite and independent cause of all the effects we see, and that cause is the God of the Bible.

Nothing can make itself. It is impossible for anything to act before it exists. That which does not understand or order itself cannot make itself. If man made himself, why did he not make himself greater than he is? Why did he limit himself to his present condition? If a toad were making himself, would he make himself a toad or a man? A man, of course! Why, then, did man stop at being man and not make himself something better? If man made himself, why does he die? Why did he not create himself to live forever? Why do new men not create themselves now?

No creature can create another creature. Otherwise, the former would be a creator and not a creature. Inventors may make new compounds, but they do not truly create—they do not start with nothing! Parents may reproduce children, but they start with an egg and a sperm. Such cannot properly be called "creating."

God created all things out of nothing. He is the first cause of every subsequent effect. He did not create Himself but is eternally and independently existent. He necessarily self-exists. There must be one original uncaused cause. Moreover, that ultimate cause must be infinitely perfect. Our knowledge of our own imperfection implies that there is such a thing as perfection. Perfection necessarily exists. That perfect person is God! Thus, Genesis chapters 1–3 alone satisfy our highest intellect with regard to the question of origins.

All Things Point to God in Their Harmony

Ink and paper did not accidentally clash to make the page you are reading. Many different hands designed and produced it. When you hear a symphony, you know that some grand composer designed the whole in all its parts. Even contrary elements are linked together in harmonious fashion. For example, water, a liquid, is composed of two gases, hydrogen and oxygen. A wise framer ordered such an arrangement. Thus, all creation in its harmony shows intelligent design behind it all.

Consider how one created object serves another created object. The sun is positioned precisely in relationship to the earth to give the right amount of heat so we neither burn to death nor freeze to death. We have the right amount of water and dry land on earth to support all the forms of life. This regularity and uniformity in all the world must have an orderer. The primitive islander who finds a clock not only admires the machine but also deduces there is a clockmaker somewhere.

Furthermore, the order and subservience in creation is constant and predictable. It is not accidental but reflects the immutability of the Creator Himself.

The variety and diversity of things in the world point to the wisdom and goodness of the Designer. He could have made everything colorless, but He gave us a whole spectrum of colors. He could have made our food tasteless, but He gave a wide variety of flavors.

All Things Point to God in Their Answering the Various Ends for Which They Were Designed

God pointed Job to various animals and their instincts to show him something of the glory of God. The Lord Jesus Christ said, "Consider the lilies" (Matt. 6:28). The plants and animals do not know their own end; they have no understanding of their own. Yet each one carries out its part in the overall scheme. Therefore, there is some superior understanding and nature that makes them act. A higher power oversees and governs them. If you see an arrow hit the bull's-eye of a target, you know that somewhere there surely is a skilled archer. But more, when you see thousands of arrows hit the bull's-eye and not one misses, there can be no doubt about the existence and skill of the archer.

All Things Point to God in Their Preservation

Nothing can preserve itself; everything depends on a higher authority for continuation. Who is the Sustainer? The psalmist tells us. "O LORD, thou preservest man and beast. . . . O LORD, how manifold are thy works! in wisdom hast thou made them all: the earth is full of thy riches. . . . These wait all upon thee; that thou mayest give them their meat in due season. That thou givest them they gather: thou openest thine hand, they are filled with good. . . . thou renewest the face of the earth" (Pss. 36:6; 104:24, 27–28, 30).

The Existence of Man Is Evidence of the Existence of God

You need look no further than the mirror to see a powerful argument for the existence of God!

Consider Your Body

Your body is "fearfully and wonderfully made" (Ps. 139:14). There is order, fitness, and usefulness in every part. Consider any organ in detail, and you will see how perfectly built it is for its purpose as it aids the rest of the body. Paul refers to this marvelous interdependence of all the parts of the body in 1 Corinthians 12. Like a fine-tuned machine, every part of us testifies to the skill of a master craftsman.

Even though we all have the same basic parts, there is wonderful difference and variety among men. Think of the individuality of fingerprints. Or think of how many combinations of eyes, nose, and mouth we find on the earth. Without this variation, we could not distinguish one person from another. One cannot help but clearly see God's hand in this.

Consider Your Soul

Your soul has a vast capacity to apprehend and talk about things far superior to itself—things that are truly out of this world. It has great faculties of reason and memory. It has quickness of motion and is capable of running through the world in a day.

There is a union of both soul and body in man, in which he is a sort of compound. If we were only spirit, we would be a kind of angel. If we were only body, we would be a kind of brute beast. We are an amazing combination of soul and clay. Dare we say that all this came of itself or of some lower form of spirit? No, it proceeded from a higher transcendent Spirit. Who but the all-wise God could devise such a scheme? Truly, a man must be ignorant of himself before he can be ignorant of the existence of God!

Consider the Operations of Your Conscience

We sense a higher judge than ourselves. All men have this "reflecting principle" in them by which they look at themselves and their neighbors. We are constantly making assessments, either accusing or excusing one another (Rom. 2:15). Every man has this inward rule of good and evil implanted in him. Wherever there is a law, there must be a lawgiver. That lawgiver is God.

Fears arise within a man when he commits evil. The closer he comes to death, the more troubled he becomes. He knows there is a higher judge than himself, and he dreads to meet Him. What other reason is there to fear death? The more secret the sin, the more the conscience convicts. This is not because others know but because a higher being knows *everything*. Men would escape this guilt if they possibly could.

Of course, a person may quiet his conscience and defile it, even sear it; but God can awaken it at any time He pleases. We have less control over our conscience than over any other faculty. Operations of conscience cannot be totally shaken off by man. "The wicked are like the troubled sea, when it cannot rest" (Isa. 57:20). He must cease to be a man who ceases to have a conscience.

On the other hand, well doing gives a person a good conscience. The consciences of other observers also approve of his well doing.

Consider the Vastness of the Desires in Man

Man is dissatisfied with everything that is below himself. We are geared to look upward, above ourselves, for something more, something perfect. We cannot find full satisfaction in that which is inferior or imperfect. Our appetite for something greater demonstrates a defect in what we presently have. Of a truth we are restless until we come to rest in God.

Unusual Occurrences Are Evidence of the Existence of God

Occurrences such as extraordinary judgments that often follow extraordinary sins demonstrate God's justice. "The LORD is known by the judgment which he executeth" (Ps. 9:16). Think of Lot's wife, who became a heap of salt, or of Herod, who was eaten by worms.

Miracles also manifest a power greater than nature itself. Nature cannot rise above itself and produce miracles. Miracles are nothing less than the finger of God. Nothing but a living God can account for such events as the resurrection of Christ from the dead.

Fulfilled prophecies bear witness to God's being. Only God in heaven, who knows all things and possesses all power, could tell beforehand what He will do, and then accomplish it in exactly that way. Scripture is full of examples of this divine arranging.

What does this doctrine mean to us? What should we learn from it?

Atheism Is a Destructive Doctrine

Atheism tends to destroy the world as a whole. The very foundations of an ordered society rest on the knowledge and fear of God. Without God, there can be no absolute standard of right and wrong. Man's conscience becomes deadened. Every man pursues his own selfish sinful desires unchecked. Man becomes a monster. Society becomes a jungle of anarchy or tyranny. Earth becomes a hell. How cruel is atheism!

Atheism destroys the atheist himself. By removing all threat of punishment and promise of reward, he is reduced to the level of a mere animal. In such a case, hope is forfeited, and all possibility of true happiness is lost. The only remaining purpose in living is momentary gratification, regardless of how unlawfully it may be achieved. On the other hand, the more conscious of God a man is, the more innocent, harmless, and useful he is in this world.

The Presence of Atheism Today Is Lamentable

Atheism is also a folly that reduces man to nothing. It removes meaning and purpose from life and leaves us with nothing but blind chance. It leaves man no longer a man at all. How sad to see educated, intelligent minds fall for the lie! But make no mistake, the devil is no atheist. Likewise, souls suffering in hell under God's judgment have no doubt concerning the existence of God now. Lest you should be deceived by the fiction of atheism, consider some further points.

No one can prove there is no God. To attempt it is absurd. Someone may object, "But I cannot see God." If we could see Him, He would no longer be infinite and, thus, no longer God at all. We cannot see the wind, but we do not doubt its operation. We still do not understand much about light, but only a fool would question its existence.

Every living thing and all of creation testifies against the atheist. Literally billions of arguments can be marshaled to refute his nonsense.

God sends special providences from time to time to act as messengers to man's conscience to keep alive the inborn notion of God. Ultimately, there can be no pure atheists. Down deep, everyone knows there is a God. Thus, in one sense, all sinners are atheists, as we said before, and in another sense, no sinner is an atheist. The so-called atheist only *wishes* there were no God and tries to live accordingly.

Men try to be atheists because they have some secret guilt, springing from a knowledge of their sin. They want to engage freely in their sin without any restraint from the thunderclaps of conscience. They pretend to throw off the yoke of slavery to God and find new freedom, but they only become slaves to sin. The only liberty the atheist gains is a liberty to defile himself. How beguiling is sin!

If the atheist is wrong, he has lost everything. If he is right, he has gained nothing. Thus, even from a merely human perspective, atheism is unreasonable.

Atheism is dishonest and makes a man an enemy to his own soul's happiness. Christians need great charity not to despise a man who despises his own soul. Though atheists are not worthy of our care, let us care for them and pity them!

If It Is Folly to Deny God's Existence, Then It Is Wisdom to Acknowledge His Existence

As Satan at first attacked the character of God in the garden of Eden, he now more boldly attacks the very being of God. But you might as well doubt your own existence as to doubt God's. He *is*.

And He is all that Scripture says He is—Lord, Governor, Sovereign over all the universe.

This knowledge is necessary to rightly worship Him. Our worship will rise only as high as our concept of God. You cannot worship one whose existence you doubt.

Without this knowledge, we cannot order our lives rightly. We will descend into every conceivable sin.

Without this knowledge, we cannot have any comfort in our lives. But with God we enjoy refuge and strength (Ps. 46:1). How could we keep our sanity in this evil world without Him? Yet, to the extent we doubt, we are comfortless.

Without this knowledge, we cannot have a firm belief in the Scripture. No God, no Bible! No Bible, no foundation for anything!

Therefore, let us study God in the creation as well as in the Scriptures. Though we see Him more clearly in the written word, we ought not neglect His evidence in nature: He is the author of both. Scripture frequently points us to nature, and neither one contradicts the other.

Also, let us see God in our own experiences of Him. Experience is a powerful teacher. Though you cannot see His essence, you can see His goodness in your own life. You will not likely doubt the existence of someone you know personally! Personal communion with God argues more for God's existence than all outward evidence in creation. There is indeed something supernatural about true Christianity, which only the renewed heart knows.

If We Believe in God's Existence Yet Deny Him Worship, We Are in the Same Folly as the Atheist

The one who professes to believe in God yet does not worship Him is an atheist to His honor, if not to His being. Since we live and move *in* Him, we should live and move *to* Him and *for* Him. It stands to reason that our noblest faculty should be engaged in the most excellent object. God should be in all our thoughts (Ps. 10:4). Therefore, remember Him always and think much upon Him. A God forgotten is as good as no God to us.

2

PRACTICAL ATHEISM

A man can have an atheistic heart without an atheistic head. He may not question the existence of God, and may even defend the same, while his heart is empty of affection toward God. This is practical atheism—that is to say, atheism in practice. The devil himself is a practical atheist: he knows there is a God but acts as if there were none. Among mankind, relatively few will absolutely deny that God exists, but no man naturally reverences God in his heart. All men are practical atheists. They are described in Titus 1:16, "They profess that they know God; but in works they deny him." Since actions speak louder than words, those who acknowledge a God but live as if there were none are more worthy of the title *atheist* than those who deny a God but live as if there were one.

This secret atheism is the spirit of all sin. Every sinful motion practically throws off God's law and sovereignty, declaring Him unworthy of His being. If it were allowed to be carried to its logical end, every sin of mankind would impugn, dethrone, and annihilate God while setting up the sinner as a wiser authority.

When we sin, we are really wishing there were no God or that He did not possess all His qualities and perfections—which would amount to there being no God. Furthermore, those who only outwardly worship because of a slavish fear, murmuring all the while, manifest the same wish. Any desire for God to change or for His dealings with us to be changed is the essence of practical atheism.

Man's problem can be summed up in two statements. Man wants to be his own god. And man seeks happiness in himself rather than in God.

Man Wants to Be His Own God

Man sets up himself as his own rule instead of God. This amounts to destroying God altogether, for God cannot exist apart from His prerogative of authority.

Man First Disowns God's Rule

Man is naturally unwilling to learn God's truth. He refuses to use the means available to him to learn about God. He casts off thoughts about God that occasionally enter his mind, wishing that the Bible did not say what it says. Any thoughts he does entertain about God stem only from carnal curiosity, not from a genuine desire to obey.

Inwardly, man in sin actively opposes the truth of God. The more he knows of God's will, the more he fights against it. The apostle describes this in Romans 7:8, "But sin, taking occasion by the commandment, wrought in me all manner of concupiscence. For without the law sin was dead." Sin within us takes advantage of our knowledge of God's law and more fiercely opposes it.

Outwardly, man persecutes those who proclaim truth. Every corner of the earth has been stained with the blood of those who stand for God and His authority. In more peaceful times, people tolerate the sound of the truth simply because it comes from the lips of a neighbor or friend.

Some practical atheists are willing to embrace some of the truth as long as they are in charge of which portion. In effect they say, "Truth that seems to be in my favor is fine, but I reserve the right to reject any truth that reproves me!"

Many people pervert God's Word to excuse their sin. For example, God's longsuffering is misconstrued as lack of concern on His part. Justification by faith is twisted into a license to sin. Christ's conversing with sinners becomes a defense for keeping evil companions. Such misuse of truth reveals that we have made our own vile affections, and not the will of God, to be our rule. This reminds us of the devil's method of twisting Scripture when he tempted Christ.

Natural man desires neither a holy God nor a holy law. Any knowledge of any thing is acceptable to him except for the knowledge of God. Why is this? Because the knowledge of God's truth humbles man, and his pride will not stand for it.

The truth that man cannot avoid he despises and holds in contempt. If he breaks any part of God's law, he shows his contempt for all of it (James 2:10). Even if he happens to keep some of God's precepts, it is only incidental and selfishly motivated; it springs not from a heart of obedience. Adam insisted on his freedom even though it was to his own hurt. Thus, all men in Adam are perfect fools. They are enemies to their own true happiness. They insist on going away from God at all costs. "Better to serve sin than to serve God" is the sinner's motto. He goes to more pains to violate God's law than he would have suffered in keeping it!

Man hates most those commands that are most spiritual, most internal, and most glorifying to God. He barely tolerates the more external, ceremonial parts of worship. He has slight thoughts of God and finds little satisfaction in Him. He must be constrained to do well and finds an abundance of excuses for not doing it. He hates to come into the presence of God and leaves as soon as he can. He offers God the leftovers. He serves God as if he were afraid that God would set up His government in his heart.

If natural man does happen to serve God in any way, it is only for some selfish interest. If God does not give what the man desires, he will desert God at once and serve Him no more. He will have God as his servant but not as his Master.

Man shows his contempt for God in the many promises he breaks. In time of distress or danger, he readily vows to God, but afterward, he relents. Thus, he proves to be the child of the father of lies (John 8:44). Could there be any clearer evidence than this of disowning God's rule?

Man Naturally Owns Any Rule Other Than That of God

Man prefers even Satan's rule to God's! Man would rather join ranks with the mortal enemy of his soul than bow to the scepter of Jehovah. By allowing such a low, wicked object to possess his heart, man shows the greatest disdain for the One who alone is worthy of it.

The more obvious rule man owns is that of man himself. The world's opinion counts with him more than anything. He complies with God's rule only when man is enforcing it, when the consequences for disobedience are too painful to endure.

Man Seeks to Set Up Himself as His Own God

Man makes an idol of his own will. Self-love and independency are the cornerstone of atheism and are the root of all sin in the world. Adam coveted equality with God. He thought to invade God's throne. Since the fall, the great controversy between God and man has been whether God or man will be God. Thank God for the second Adam who did not cling to His divine privileges but humbled Himself and came to earth and died (Phil. 2:5–8) to undo what the first Adam had done!

When a man sins, his conscience accuses him, so he seeks to eradicate it. He does not like to retain any knowledge of the true God (Rom. 1:28). This is a great evil, for destroying conscience is equal to destroying God. It is His messenger.

The apparent good natural man does is only *relatively* good because he does it to please himself rather than to honor God. He does what is good only because his will happens to coincide with

God's on that point. The ruling principle in his soul, however, is clearly not God but self. Reputation before men or some other selfish advantage motivates the man. Thus, what appears to us as obedience to God is often really disobedience in the eyes of God.

When a man charts out his course of action without considering God's Word and will in the matter, he acts as his own god. He would rather displease God than displease himself. The practical atheist effectively becomes his own sovereign.

Ultimately, Man Wants to Be a God to God

Man wants to be almighty over the Almighty. As long as God will walk by our rule, we will acknowledge Him. We are willing for God to be our benefactor but not our ruler. We want to mint a new, improved God. But such a God is a fantasy, existing only in our imagination. God says to us, "Thou thoughtest that I was altogether such an one as thyself" and this really amounts to *forgetting God* (Ps. 50:21–22). Consider some ways in which man reconstructs God in his imagination.

❖ When we strive against God's holy law, we set up ourselves as God. We effectively say, "I know better than God what is good for me." God has the right to dictate law to His creatures. But we pretend to dictate law to God whenever we disagree with His commandment.

❖ When we disapprove of God's government of His world, we set up ourselves as God. It is as if God had to give an account to us, as if we, and not He, were the ones really concerned about problems. We set up ourselves as God's teachers and counselors. We imagine that He is the one at fault, never ourselves.

❖ When we are impatient under difficulties, we imagine our wisdom and righteousness and timing are better than

God's. We think ourselves to be superior to Him in ordering providence.

❖ When we envy others, we betray a heart set against God. We say, "God did not consult with me as to His dispensing of His gifts. He owes me this or that."

❖ When we pray selfishly, demanding of God what He has not promised nor determined to give us, we evidence great sinful pride. We pray as though we were determined to bring God down to our terms.

❖ When we hastily or carelessly interpret God's providence in some unusual judgment, we fasten our own will as a law or motive upon God. For example, in Luke 13, Christ warned against precipitously assuming that the Galileans, whom Pilate had slain, to be greater sinners than others. Let us be cautious how we interpret afflictions that come upon our enemies.

❖ When we disregard God's regulative principle in worship, introducing our own novelties that please and appeal to man, we practically throw God off His throne.

❖ When we twist Scripture to our liking rather than to follow the intention of the mind of God, we make ourselves to be more authoritative than God.

❖ Any who turn back from following Christ when troubles arise practically deify themselves. Personal ease and covetousness become their God. They think they are better judges than God of what is truly profitable.

We could add to the list: ingratitude, stubbornness, and the like. But the sum of it all is this: the practical atheist becomes a god unto himself.

Man Sets Up Himself as His Own End and Happiness Instead of God

God deserves our highest esteem. We ought to both depend on Him and enjoy Him. But in our natural state, we attempt to reverse all of this.

As Man Brings God Down, He Sets Himself Up

Our sinful self-love plays a deadly role here. We should understand that there are three kinds of self-love, which may be designated as *nature*, *sin*, and *grace*. First, God has implanted in every person a natural self-love. Our instinctive self-preservation evidences this kind of love. Without it, we are not men at all. Second, sinful man possesses a carnal self-love, whereby he exalts himself above God. This is inordinate self-love, the sinful excess of the natural self-love. Third, in a state of grace, a man comes to love his soul's best interest. Honoring God becomes his chief delight. Earthly, temporal concerns become subservient to those of his soul. The second kind of self-love is the one involved in practical atheism. Sin appeals to us on the grounds of self-satisfaction. We view sin as good for us. Living for sin equals living for self. Even in religion, carnal self-love may motivate us. For example, we may give our body to be burned as a martyr, but if we do so with unsanctified affections, there is no profit (1 Cor. 13:3).

In what ways does a man make himself his own end?

❖ By applauding himself and embracing himself and dwelling on his own perceived perfections rather than God's.

❖ By ascribing glory and honor to himself, taking credit for any good he does and blaming God for any problem.

❖ By insisting on doctrines that please him and hiring a false prophet to teach them.

❖ By having greater concern for injuries committed against himself than for those committed against God.

❖ By trusting himself and his own wit and wisdom rather than seeking God's mind.

❖ By violating conscience, which is God's deputy, to please himself.

In these and many other ways, we prove ourselves practical atheists.

We usurp God's prerogative, making ourselves our own end. We defame God, insinuating He is not as worthy of our love as are we ourselves. We practically destroy God, inasmuch as we can, by denying Him His revealed will and honor in our lives.

Man Will Set Up Most Anything Except God in Place of God

Only an irrational being would do such a thing formally or explicitly, but all men by nature do this virtually and implicitly. Man foolishly imagines he can be content without God. Instead of having God in all his thoughts, he has God in hardly any (Ps. 10:4). He has fewer thoughts of God than of most anything else. He finds no delight in God as God. He eagerly and greedily pursues worldly interests. He is addicted to the pleasures of the flesh and pawns the pleasures of God, in which angels delight, for the sake of earthly gratification. He praises the means or instrument rather than the source of all his blessings. He treats God as a mere spectator in his life. He debases God by setting up some creature or some sin as God in his life. In all, he denies God at every turn.

Man Makes Himself the End of All Creatures

So selfish are we by nature, we think we are worthy not only of our own supreme affection but also of that of others. We imagine we are the end for which all else exists. Though some may work to conceal it, all men have this lofty opinion of themselves.

Man Makes Himself the End for Which God Exists

Man would make even God subject to man! How does man do this? In many subtle ways, as the following examples show:

❖ Man would make God his end by loving God only for selfish reasons, only when God grants him some benefit. This is but to love the gift but not the Giver.

❖ Man would make God his end by abstaining from certain sins only because doing so helps to promote some other sinful purpose. For example, he may abstain from drunkenness only to preserve his body for himself. Not the fear of God but some self-serving interest motivates the practical atheist.

❖ Man would make God his end by performing religious duties purely for personal gain. How many atheists wear a thin mask of religion! If there is no evident profit for himself, he is slack to perform any duty. If he could manage without God, he gladly would. He only prays in time of personal affliction and need. Prayer is often most fervent when it is least godly. The practical atheist only asks God to rubber-stamp his personal self-centered schemes. He grows impatient when God does not answer his prayers nor operate on his time schedule.

❖ Man would make God his end by aiming at a selfish goal when he does do some religious duties. Simon the sorcerer would gladly exercise miraculous gifts if by so doing he could receive recognition and honor from men (Acts 8). Those who come to Christ only to escape hell, having no positive desire for holiness and for God's glory, are likewise woefully guilty here. Do we hate sin primarily because it hurts us or because it offends God? The motivation behind all our obedience comes into question. For example, do we maintain family worship only for bragging rights? In all things, we must keep God's evaluation of us in view and seek His honor and glory.

❖ Man would make God his end by using God as an excuse for sin. Man leans on some twisted interpretation of Scripture as a crutch to support his lusts. For example, "Use a little wine for thy stomach's sake" (1 Tim. 5:23) is often quoted by drunkards. This is to make God in agreement with sin and exhibits a high degree of atheism.

We See Further Evidence of Practical Atheism in That Man Holds Unworthy Views of God

Man wants to reduce God to a manageable size. This small God can be satisfied with small justice, small holiness, and small obedience. Superstition soon arises. Men begin to treat God like a baby, flattering Him, bribing Him. Then they imagine God's threats to be empty, intended only to scare men. All this is simply mental idolatry and is the common spiritual disease of the whole world. If an accurate picture of this god could be portrayed, what a monster would appear on the canvas!

Such thoughts about God are vicious and defaming. They are worse than idolatry. They make God to be not only a creature but a sinful one at that. They are even worse than absolute atheism. Better to deny His existence than to deny His perfection.

Man's natural avoidance of God demonstrates his practical atheism. He loathes God simply because He is holy, pure, and perfect. Man has no interest in imitating God in holiness. Man pays attention to every little thing except the great God. He desires no communication with God. The louder God calls, the more man runs away.

Information

Of what use is this teaching to us?

God Is Exceedingly Patient and Merciful

God continues to give life and breath to His sworn enemies, who continually provoke Him. They would have killed Him long ago, yet He preserves them. He has even determined to save a great multitude of them. What a God!

God Is Justified in Exercising Justice against His Enemies

We are guilty of spiritual treason and ought to be destroyed. Because we have sinned against the infinite God, our guilt is infinite, and we deserve infinite punishment.

We Need a New Nature within Us to Avoid Our Natural Atheism

An evil disposition is seated in our nature. It is not a minor wound but a disease that has corrupted us through and through. We need a whole new principle of life deep within us. Only then can we love God supremely.

How Difficult Is Conversion from Sin and Subsequent Mortification of Sin

Indeed, it is impossible with men. Is it an easy thing for a man to turn his arms against himself and overthrow his own empire? True conversion is radical as well as painful. Living a holy life is not child's play. It goes against all we know and are by nature.

Here We Discover the Reason Why Men Persist in Unbelief

The gospel utterly humbles us. In the gospel, God is all in all. Men would naturally prefer the law, which tells them to do something, rather than the gospel, which tells us that God in Christ has done it all. The very essence of faith requires us to renounce ourselves and look to Christ for righteousness.

God Alone Is the Author of Grace and of Every Good Work

We are slaves to our own sinful nature. Every person who ever turned to God was first turned by God. In redemption, we are debtors to mercy alone, debtors to pure and sovereign grace.

The Best Works of Man Cannot Justify Him

We cannot rise above ourselves. As natural men, our best works are but expressions of some atheistic thought, desire, or motive. Our neighbors may praise us as good people, but they cannot see our heart.

Practical Atheism Is the Cause of All Apostasy from a Christian Profession

Secretly, the apostate never fully submitted to God's rule in his life. He was determined to have praise, pleasure, or some personal profit above all else.

The Excellence of True Christianity

It sets man down in a low place, where he belongs, while it exalts God to the highest throne, where He belongs. The gospel puts man in the dust, from whence he came, and glorifies the eternal God as God. The light of nature may conquer absolute atheism, but only the light of the gospel conquers practical atheism.

Exhortation

What should our response be to the evil of practical atheism?

Let Us Be Humbled for Our Practical Atheism

We must be aware of it in ourselves and in others. None of us are natural lovers of God. How frequently have we neglected Him! How diligently we pursue any object except Him! How slack we are to serve such a good God! Was there ever a more practically atheistic society than the present one? What must God see when He looks down from heaven upon earth and into our very hearts!

Practical atheism is simply unreasonable. It inverts the order of reality. It holds God in contempt and prefers some created thing instead. When we sin, we act as if sin were really our God. To deny the Highest His due is the lowest depth of sin. By virtue of who He is, He is worthy of all our affection, worship, and service.

Consider how much ingratitude resides in practical atheism. Suppose a great benefactor lived in the same house with a man and yet that man never exchanged a word with the one who sustained him, never offered a token of thanksgiving. "How evil!" you say. But is this not how we deal with God? This is worse than what the devil does. His defiance is more excusable because he is expressly under condemnation while God daily loads us with benefits. We regard God as if He were likely to do us wrong, when in reality He always does what is perfectly right. Our ingratitude is a shameful insult to God.

The end of such a course against God is sure to be eternal misery. Whoever is ambitious to be his own heaven will at last find his soul to become its own hell. In hell the atheist gets, in some sense, what he craved: to be left to himself. But he will discover it to be torment and not joy.

Let Every Believer in Christ Mortify the Practical Atheism That Remains in Him

Sin is a turning from God to self. We need to ask only two questions in every action: "Is God's will my rule?" and "Is God's glory my end?" All sin is the neglect of these considerations. All grace is the practice of them. To help us mortify practical atheism, consider the following simple rules.

Pray much to God and meditate much on Him. We must stay near to God. Distance is the first step to disaffection. Daily communion with God makes us delight in Him and detest any thought of offending Him. All sin begins by failure in our prayer closet.

Prize and study the Scripture. How can we delight in God if we do not know Him? How can we know Him but by His Word? If you would not throw off God as your rule, do not throw off Scripture as your guide.

Take heed to sensual pleasures. We must practice self-denial and a moderate use of earthly comforts. Nothing is more apt to quench our appetite for God than addiction to worldly pleasures. Beware of this great snare!

Guard against presumptuous sins. In other words, do not sin against knowledge, but walk in all the light you see. When you deliberately sin, your soul becomes fertile soil for the growth of a fatal crop of practical atheism.

3

GOD IS A SPIRIT

The woman at the well of Samaria in John 4 was a practical atheist who "worshiped" God. Like her, we are all willing to acknowledge God but refuse to live lives in conformity to His revealed will. In correcting the errors of the woman, our Lord pointed out that her worship was wrong because her understanding of God was wrong. To worship God rightly, we must know something of who He is. His nature is the foundation of our worship.

If God were corporeal, He might be satisfied with corporeal worship. But "God is spirit" (John 4:24), and therefore we must worship Him with our spirit. The involvement of the physical body in worship is secondary. Primary is the affectionate motion of our heart.

The New Testament time is more suited to the nature of God than any other. Certainly, the true worshipers in the Old Testament possessed the Holy Spirit, otherwise they could never have worshiped. But in the New Testament time, there is a fuller outpouring of the Holy Spirit. Thus, it is called "the administration of the Spirit" (2 Cor. 3:8).

Furthermore, our Lord taught that we must worship God *in truth*. He is not here contrasting truth with lies, for even in the Old Testament time God required truth. "Behold, thou desirest truth in the inward parts" (Ps. 51:6). Rather, the Lord is contrasting truth with the types and shadows of the Old Testament. Truth is the object that cast those shadows.

Since God is God, worship is due to Him. Since God is spirit, the worship due Him must be of a spiritual sort. In other words, our worship of God must agree with His mode of existence.

God Has No Body

A body would take away from God's majestic excellence. Among mankind, we find that our spirit is nobler than our body. It acts alone. Our body, however, cannot act alone nor live alone; it must have our spirit to enliven and activate it.

Our spirit is our principal part. Being made in the likeness of God has reference to that part of our nature that is most elevated—namely, our spirit. Since the Creator exceeds the creature in all things, so He exceeds us in His mode of existence: He has nothing material in His essence.

To say that God is a spirit is truly a negation. Most of what we know about God we know in terms of negation—what He is not like. As physical beings, we can hardly conceive of the existence of any person apart from that which is material. So, when God tells us He is spirit, we understand Him to say that He is unlike us. Nor should we equate His spirit with the angels' spirits, which are finite. God is infinitely higher than any of His creation.

God Is a Spirit

If He had a body, He could not charge mankind with the sin of changing His glory into an image made like to corruptible man, birds, beasts, or creeping things (Rom. 1:23). He is truly "the Father of spirits" (Heb. 12:9). Consider what would be true if God existed in any other mode.

If God Were Not a Spirit, He Could Not Be Creator

Creation is complex. All complexity must begin in simplicity. All multitude must originate in solitude. The simple, supreme Divine

Spirit is the source of all the effects we see in creation.

If God Were Not a Spirit, He Could Not Be One Essence

If He had a body, He would be a compound—composed of various parts and able to be divided. Each part would either be finite or infinite. If finite, the parts would be unworthy of God. If infinite, each part would be God, and thus, there would be many Gods. But God is no composite; He is one: "Hear, O Israel: The Lord our God is one Lord" (Deut. 6:4).

If God Were Not a Spirit, He Could Not Be Invisible

Invisibility is one of His perfections. "Now unto the King eternal, immortal, invisible" (1 Tim. 1:17). Things visible are within our grasp, but things invisible are beyond us. As God is invisible to our sense, so He is incomprehensible to our understanding. When He is said to have appeared to Moses and other prophets, they did not see His very essence, but they saw a form suited to their limited capacity of perception. No mortal man can see God (Ex. 33:20). If He were corporeal, we might see Him in some measure.

If God Were Not a Spirit, He Could Not Be Infinite

One of the biggest things we know is the sun, yet even it can be measured. It has its limitations. But God has no boundaries: "The heaven and heaven of heavens cannot contain him" (2 Chron. 2:6).

If God Were Not a Spirit, He Could Not Be Independent

A compound substance depends on the integration of its parts for its existence. If the parts are separated, the substance ceases to be. We assume the parts to have an existence of their own before they come together. If God were thus composed, He would be dependent on the preexisting inferior parts and their synthesis for His being. But nothing is before Him. He is the first and the last (Isa. 44:6). This can only be true if He is a pure, simple spirit.

If God Were Not a Spirit, He Could Not Be Immutable

Whatever is compounded from parts may be divided into those parts. This is what occurs when a man dies. His life is composed of body and spirit, but those parts divide, and a lifeless corpse is left on the earth. But God, being an unmixed spirit, admits of no division and of no change.

If God Were Not a Spirit, He Could Not Be Omnipresent

God fills heaven and earth (Jer. 23:24). But a corporeal mode of existence would make this impossible, for a body can be in only one place at a time. If God were both omnipresent and corporeal, there would be no room left for any of us; God would fill every space. Nor would there be room left for any motion whatsoever; no place would remain for the motion to occur. God would be immobile.

If God Were Not a Spirit, He Could Not Be the Most Perfect Being

Instead, angels and disembodied souls of men would be more excellent than He, seeing they are not cumbered with bodies. But He transcends us in excellence to an infinite degree as the Divine Spirit.

Some may question, "If God is a spirit, what about the body parts mentioned in Scripture, such as His heart, arms, hands, eyes, ears, and face?" In answer, consider several points. First, He condescends to our weakness in His descriptions of Himself. We can only conceive of God in terms with which we, as men, are familiar. Second, these body parts express God's visible operations, not His invisible nature. There is some correspondence in the divine operation and the organ we associate with a similar operation in our own body. For example, His eyes refer to His omniscience, and His arm refers to His power. Third, only man's noblest parts and activities are employed in describing God. Organs having to do with getting knowledge, communicating knowledge, and manifesting power are used with reference to God but never lower senses that pertain only to corporeal actions. Fourth, the Old Testament descriptions and appearances of God served to foreshadow the incarnation of God the Son. Fifth, we are to think of the body parts according to the metaphor, not according to the letter. Otherwise, we are forced to think of God as a bird since we read of His wings. The Scriptures use many such metaphors.

What should we learn from this teaching?

Man's Being Made in God's Image Does Not Involve Physical Faculties

After all, we share physical qualities with the animals, but none of them are made in God's image. God's image in man refers to such faculties as reason, understanding, and an immortal spirit. Our soul is the faculty that comes nearest to the nature of God.

It Is Unreasonable to Make Any Image of God

Idolatry attempts the impossible. "To whom then will ye liken God? Or what likeness will ye compare unto him?" (Isa. 40:18). Nothing corporeal can adequately represent a spiritual substance. Only God fully knows Himself; only He can adequately reveal Himself. But He has not revealed Himself with any physical form. No carving or painting can do justice to His glorious character. Any representation is finite and must leave out something. Thus, any representation becomes a misrepresentation. This is unworthy of Him and amounts to an insult against Him.

Nevertheless, man in sin is naturally prone to make a representation of God. From the most ancient post-flood times, men have insisted on some image or form in connection with religious

worship. This is idolatry and is expressly and repeatedly condemned
in Holy Scripture. "We ought not to think that the Godhead is like
unto gold, or silver, or stone, graven by art and man's device" (Acts
17:29). When we use an image in worship, we either worship the
image itself or the object it represents. The former is overt idolatry.
The latter is foolishness, for it makes the image not necessary at all.

The Spirituality of God Should Govern Our Whole Concept of God

We should be content not to have any picture or image of Him. He
is beyond us. He is infinite. Even the elect angels must be content
not to know God fully. Yet He stoops down to reveal something of
Himself to us.

We must understand how great an evil is idolatry. We deny
God's spirituality when we think of Him with a bodily form. We
debase Him by making Him in our image and likeness. In our
minds we limit that which is infinite. Even the most beautiful
painting detracts from His glory. Soon the viewers will begin to
ascribe a corrupt nature to God. But God's humbling Himself to
our apprehensions by using figurative language is no reason for us
to degrade Him by thinking He actually exists in those figures. The
human qualities attributed to God are suited to our weakness more
than to His perfection.

Idolatry spoils true worship. We will not seriously address a
God of whom we have a low view. The higher our view of God, the
more we are humbled and abhor ourselves before Him. We ought to
have elevated notions of God. Due to our finiteness, we cannot have
a full view of Him, but we should endeavor to have the loftiest view
possible. We must remember that no matter how high a knowledge
of Him we attain, He is even higher than this!

Some Inferences from This Doctrine

If God is a spirit, no corporeal object can defile Him. No filth of flesh can come into contact with Him.

If God is a spirit, He is not bogged down with a mass of size and weight but is free to act, even in our souls. He does not tire from overwork. The more like God we are, the more active we will be for His glory.

If God is a spirit, He is immortal. Death is always separation. Since God is a simple uncompounded spirit, there can be no separation in Him. This truth is a great comfort to the children of God.

If God is a spirit, we have a capacity to hold communion with Him in our spirits. "The sacrifices of God are a broken spirit" (Ps. 51:17). Therefore, we need to be renewed in the spirit of our minds (Eph. 4:23).

If God is a spirit, only He can satisfy our spirits. Nothing physical can satisfy the hungry spirit. We should have a spiritual longing for Him. Only in Him do we find rest, contentment, and fullness.

If God is a spirit, we ought to take more care for our spirits than our bodies. How often we live as if our physical substance were our all. Christianity makes a man concerned chiefly for his spirit.

If God is a spirit, we must be on guard especially against sins of the spirit. "Let us cleanse ourselves from all filthiness of the flesh and spirit, perfecting holiness in the fear of God" (2 Cor. 7:1). Sins of the flesh are wicked, indeed, and worthy of eternal wrath from God, but sins of the spirit are especially evil in that they defile that which is nearest to God in us. Sins of the flesh make us like a brute beast, but sins of the spirit make us like a devil. Just as spirituality is the root of other perfections in God (as we previously listed), so holiness of spirit in us is the root of other obedience in our flesh.

4

SPIRITUAL WORSHIP

In the last chapter, we laid the groundwork for the present subject. Since God is a spirit, the worship that is due Him must be of a spiritual nature, from our spirits. Again, the words of our Lord to the woman of Samaria in John 4:24 apply: "God is a Spirit: and they that worship him must worship him in spirit and in truth." We are not to use the ceremonies of the Jews, prescribed in the Old Testament, nor of the Samaritans, derived from various sources. The latter were false, and the former have been replaced by the New Testament order.

At all times, true worship to God has consisted chiefly in a spiritual and sincere frame. Worship must suit the nature of the object worshiped. There must be some proportion between God and the manner whereby we adore Him. If He were a body, images and physical motions might suffice. But because He is a spirit, we do not seek a loud voice so much as an elevated soul; not so much a bended knee as a broken heart; not so much an affected sound as a groaning spirit. The New Testament economy is especially well suited to true spiritual worship.

Some Propositions Concerning Spiritual Worship

Before going any further, let us make some general observations about spiritual worship.

The Spirituality of God Is the Ground of Our Worship

His being a spirit declares what He is; His other perfections declare what kind of spirit He is. Therefore, whether we adore His goodness or patience or justice or wisdom, or any other facet of His glorious character, it is His being a spirit that governs *how* we adore Him. His mode of being is the rule of worship. This should safeguard us from descending into merely carnal worship.

Nature Teaches Us That Worship Must Be Spiritual

The ceremonial forms of worship God required had to be communicated from God to man, but man instinctively knows that the worship he brings must be more than ceremonial and external. Even idolaters never claim to be worshiping the idol but rather what the idol represents. We all know that our highest faculties, with which we contemplate God, must be used in the worship of God. Romans 1 teaches that in perverting worship, man goes against his better understanding. Idolatry is not a sin of ignorance but a sin against light.

God Has Always Required Spiritual Worship

This applied to man even in Paradise before the fall. Also, before the commencement of the New Testament order, God commanded His people to love Him with all their hearts and to circumcise their hearts.

It Is as Much Our Duty to Worship God in Spirit as to Worship Him at All

We sin as much by not worshiping God rightly as by not worshiping Him at all. He deserves our highest and best. If our spirit is not engaged but only our body, we present a dead sacrifice to God.

The Ceremonial Worship of the Old Testament Was Abolished to Promote Spiritual Worship

Spiritual worship was veiled under a thick cloud of material objects, which touched the senses of the flesh. That economy is called "the oldness of the letter" (Rom. 7:6). In it, "the children of Israel could not stedfastly look to the end of that which is abolished" (2 Cor. 3:13). Carnal ceremonies were never able to bring the hearts of men into a spiritual frame. They could not perfect the worshipers nor purge the conscience. Just as a man's shadow cannot perform what the man himself can do because it lacks life, even so these shadows could only point to a better economy. They could not change the heart. We could even argue that they tended more to hinder than to encourage spiritual worship, due to the weakness of the people. Their preoccupation with things material led to their expectations of a carnal Messiah and kingdom. Here Israel stumbled. They choked on the shell and missed the kernel.

God testified that He was not pleased with the ceremonial type of worship and sometimes seems to have been weary of the institutions that He himself had ordained: "I am full of the burnt offerings of rams, and the fat of fed beasts; and I delight not in the blood of bullocks, or of lambs, or of he goats" (Isa. 1:11). God never intended that the old economy should endure but often mentioned it would be replaced by one that was more durable: a new covenant. The Lord Jesus Christ ratified this covenant in His work of redemption.

The New Covenant Is More Spiritual in Its Worship than the Old Covenant

It is a state of more grace and more truth (John 1:17). The perfections of God are revealed more clearly. We worship Him through His Son. The Holy Spirit is more plentifully poured out. We engage in a reasonable service.

There Is a Place for Our Body in the Worship of God

All our faculties are for Him. We are commanded to "glorify God in your body, and in your spirit, which are God's" (1 Cor. 6:20). Since public worship is ordained of God, physical dimensions of worship are required, such as being present, singing, praying, hearing, or preaching. Our spiritual motions must have a vent in the outward members of the body. The Lord is our supreme example in this matter: He prayed sometimes kneeling, sometimes lifting up His eyes.

That Which Constitutes Spiritual Worship

The whole soul of man must be employed in this glorious privilege. Our mind must be full of thoughts of God. "Sing ye praises with understanding" (Ps. 47:7). Our affections must perceive Him to be altogether lovely. Our will must be moved to adore, reverence, and embrace Him. There cannot be the exercise of true religion where there is not an exercise of the rational faculties. Let us mark several particulars concerning spiritual worship.

Spiritual Worship Must Stem from a Spiritual Nature

That is, the worshiper must be renewed by the Spirit of God; he must be given a new nature by God. For a beast to act like a man, he must have a man's nature implanted in him. Likewise, spiritual acts cannot be performed without Christ in the soul. We must make sure we are not merely united to a religious duty but that we are savingly united to Christ.

Spiritual Worship Is Possible Only by the Influence and Assistance of the Holy Spirit of God

We cannot mortify any sin nor quicken any service but by the enabling of the indwelling Holy Spirit. We are unable to move ourselves until He raises our faculties to a pitch agreeable to God. True prayer is that which is offered in the Spirit: "praying in the Holy Ghost" (Jude 20).

Spiritual Worship Is Done with Sincerity of Heart

God says, "My son, give me thine heart" (Prov. 23:26). Like Paul the apostle, we must serve God with our spirit in the gospel of His Son (Rom. 1:9). Without the heart, worship is only a charade. Without the heart, the tongue is a liar. We might as well expect God to delight in mere bodily worship as for ourselves to enjoy conversing with a carcass.

Spiritual Worship Must Be Performed with a United Heart

As the union of all our body parts is the life of the body, so the moral union of our hearts is the life of our worship. We ought to pray with David, "Unite my heart to fear thy name" (Ps. 86:11). O that we might say with David, "With my whole heart have I sought thee" (Ps. 119:10)! A divided heart spoils worship. All our thoughts ought to be ravished with God. In worship we must shut the door, keeping company with Christ and excluding all intruders.

Spiritual Worship Must Be Performed with a Fervent, Intense Spirit

Our understanding and will should be active. Our spirits should be enlarged. The excellence of the One we worship demands our highest engagement of strength. Drowsy worship does not become Him! The things of God ought to stimulate us more than any earthly things. Our souls must be boiling hot when we serve the Lord. One of the terms of Scripture used to designate our service to God is *agonizomai*, from which we derive the English word *agonize*. This intensity of worship must not be measured by external excitement. Let us beware of substituting outward motion in place of inward. Our body may be hot, while our souls are frozen. In the highest raptures of our spirits, our bodies are most uninvolved.

Spiritual Worship Must Be Performed from a Principle of Grace Within the Soul

Every grace unites in a believer to send forth fountains of worship. If reason alone were all that were necessary, then all rational creatures would be Christians. But there must be more. Grace does not exclude reason but ennobles it. To worship only with our body makes us act like beasts. To worship only with our reason makes us act like men. But to worship with our grace is to worship spiritually, as Christians. Since God is the author of our graces, it is only fit that He should receive of them again.

Christian graces come as a package—either all or none. Though they admit of degrees in individuals, yet they all must be present in some measure in every child of God. Consider some graces necessary in order to worship God truly.

Faith is necessary in spiritual worship. How can we worship a God in whom we have no confidence? Unbelief hinders us from any spiritual duty. Unbelief renders as dead any outward service we bring to God.

Love is necessary in spiritual worship. In the New Testament economy, the worship of God is more often expressed by love than by fear. In the law, God had more the garb of a judge; in the gospel, God has more the garb of a father. His goodness evokes in us a fear: not a sense of terror, but of reverence. The law is stripped of its cursing power and made sweet in the blood of the Redeemer. All the devotion we owe God is summed up in this word, found in both Testaments, "Thou shalt love the LORD thy God with all thine heart."

A knowledge of our own weakness is necessary in spiritual worship. The more we adore God, the more we abhor ourselves. The more we delight in Him, the more we grieve over ourselves. Worship both elevates as well as melts. True worshipers identify with the publican who cried out for mercy, not with the Pharisee who boasted that he was better than other men.

Spiritual desires for God are necessary in spiritual worship. We hunger and thirst, pant and follow hard after Him. Our desires are for nothing less than God Himself. We long to behold His beauty and taste the ravishing sweetness of His presence. A carnal worshiper may desire worship as an end in itself; but a spiritual worshiper desires it as a means to commune with the living God.

Thankfulness and admiration are necessary in spiritual worship. Praise to God in the heart is essential to true gospel worship. We should especially praise Him for His works of redemption, which rise above even the works of creation.

Delight is necessary in spiritual worship. A sad frame of heart precludes worship and contradicts all that the gospel proclaims. Aaron and his two surviving sons could not perform the priestly duties while grieving over the death of the other sons and brothers. There must be melody in our hearts to the Lord. God loves a cheerful giver. Where there is no delight in a duty, there is no delight in the object of the duty.

At the same time, deep reverence is necessary in spiritual worship. Again, the gospel removes the terror, but not the reverence toward God. Even the angels, who have no sin for which to be ashamed, cover their faces before Him. The fallen angels have a slavish fear, but redeemed men have a "godly fear" (Heb. 12:28). Toward us, God lays aside His justice, but He does not lay aside His majesty.

Humility is necessary in spiritual worship. High thoughts of God tend to make low thoughts of self. The departure of men and angels from God began in pride, and our approaches and return to Him must begin in humility.

Holiness is necessary in spiritual worship. "Holiness becometh thine house, O Lord, for ever" (Ps. 93:5). God's holiness is the basis of our worship; shall we worship Him without any concern to be like Him? How can we praise His purity while we insist on remaining defiled? The hands lifted up to God must be "holy hands" (1 Tim. 2:8).

A right aim and end are necessary to spiritual worship, namely, the glory of God. He must be the object of our worship. There are wrong reasons for worshiping, such as to be seen of men. Pharisees make an idol of themselves in their professed worship of God. Our worship is spiritual when we have the same end in view as God has: His own glory.

Spiritual worship must be offered up in the name of Christ. We recognize that even our best attempts at worship are not acceptable outside of Christ our Mediator. God outside of Christ is a dreadful thought for Adam's fallen race. But in Christ, God is more a father than a judge to us.

Why God Is Due Spiritual Worship

As we pursue this subject, we must understand both God and man—the worshiped and the worshiper, the object and the subject.

We Must Worship God Spiritually Because He Is Worthy of Our Best

We cannot give Him all He deserves, but we must give Him the best we have to offer: the best of our affections, the flower of our strength, the cream of our spirits. Nothing we have is too good for God. Under the Old Testament, God left us an example by requiring the best animals for sacrifice. Even pagans offered their best when they burned their precious children for Moloch. Their zeal puts ours to shame! Moreover, God gives us His best—His beloved and only begotten Son—as a sacrifice for us. How can we begrudge God the choicest part of ourselves?

We Must Worship God Spiritually Because Reason Demands It

Having been created with faculties of reason, thought, and a capacity to commune with God, we ought to employ these in their highest use. Not to be a spiritual worshiper reduces us to the level of brute beasts or, no doubt, even worse, because the animals fulfill the end for which they were created with their capacities.

We Must Worship God Spiritually Because Without an Engaged Spirit, No Act Is Truly an Act of Worship

Our spirit is the essential part of worship, without which other motions are dead works and a mockery of worship. We may as well say a corpse in a church building is worshiping God as to say that a living body with a dull spirit in a church building is worshiping Him.

We Must Worship God Spiritually Because in Worship, God Approaches Man

Thus, we read in Scripture of God's special presence with His people. If God stoops down to meet with us, ought we not to be present with our most spiritual capacity? How can we expect His heart, when we do not give Him ours? God and His worship are closely linked; you cannot honor one while slighting the other.

We Must Worship God Spiritually Because This Is the End for Which God Has Redeemed Us

He gives us a holy nature so that we might know and adore Him and be like Him and draw near to Him. We can no more be worshipers of God without a worshiper's nature than a man can be a man without a man's nature. God first gave Adam the privilege of worship, and in redemption He restores that privilege again.

We Must Worship God Spiritually Because This Is the Only Worship Acceptable to God

Our great concern must be to be acceptable to God. We are expressly told that our "spiritual sacrifices [are] acceptable to God by Jesus Christ" (1 Peter 2:5). How unacceptable must that worship be that is not spiritually suited to the nature of God! Would a man be happy with a bottle of water from one whose cellar was full of wine? A spiritual frame is more pleasing to God than the highest outward adornments, gifts, or knowledge.

Information

Let us now consider what we should learn from this doctrine. How sad to see so many people not truly worshiping God! Many go through outward rituals while their hearts are far from God. Their worship is as good as none at all.

Worship is a duty incumbent upon all men by virtue of creation. To neglect it demonstrates a high degree of atheism. We might even argue that worshiping a false god is not as evil as worshiping none whatsoever.

We should not be content with mere outward worship. Oftentimes, people will try to make up for a lack of heart by giving greater diligence to external manners in worship. But outward manners are no substitute for inward matter. Just as sin is primarily a heart attitude, so likewise is worship. Even in the Old Testament, the blood of animals alone meant nothing to God.

Examination

We are warned against those who have a form of godliness but deny the power thereof. It behooves us to make sure we are not guilty of form-only worship. Do we prepare our hearts to worship? Are we content to prepare our bodies only? How much do we resemble

Pharisees in focusing on formalities while neglecting spiritual concerns? Are our hearts fixed on God? When we should be worshiping, do we allow our minds to wander into lesser concerns or even sinful thoughts? Do we think God should be happy with superficial devotion from us? Are we stirred in our depths by thoughts of God? Do we worship with a servile fear or a holy fear? Is our worship forced, or do we know something of freedom and spontaneity with God? After worship, do our spirits glow, as did Moses' face? Do we find grace strengthened and sin weakened? Are we left humbler? Do we have happy reflections about the time we spent in worship? Are we eager for more of God?

Comfort

The smallest act springing from a sincere heart is worth more than great acts without heart. God rewards the simple giving of a cup of cold water, if we give from a spiritual motivation.

Sadly, every believer struggles with impurity of heart in worship. Our remaining natural corruption causes hindrances, distractions, and interruptions. Sin fights for its life when we are at worship. Sin and worship are mortal enemies: either sin must die, or worship will. Also, Satan hinders us from worshiping God. He separated from God and seeks to separate us from God as well.

These difficulties in worship should not lead us to conclude that we have no grace at all. Instead, God may accomplish some good purpose in us through them. First, He may humble us. If we could worship perfectly in our present state, we might be lifted up with pride. We need thorns in our spirit, if not in our flesh, to keep us humble. Nothing is so dangerous as spiritual pride. Second, God allows hindrances in worship in order to make us prize it highly. If it were not such a good thing, Satan would not oppose it so fiercely. We should value worship more when we see what a threat our enemy considers it to be. Third, we admire God all the more when we consider that He accepts any worship from us at all. It is so full of imperfection—yet God is so gracious as to receive it! Fourth, hindrances in worship should make us appreciate Christ our Mediator all the more. He stands between us and the infirmities of our worship. We recognize all the more our utter dependence on the Savior of our souls; we trust Him more fully than ever. Thus, the purpose of God is fulfilled, and the purpose of Satan is defeated.

Therefore, we should not let our hindrances in worship discourage us. They prove our true heart by our resistance to them. They make us watch more carefully. They make Christ's intercession more precious to us.

Exhortation

Since God respects the disposition of the sacrificer more than the multitude of the sacrifices, let us strive above all else to be true spiritual worshipers. The devil requires hearty obedience from those whom he deceives. Should our dedication to God be any less? Consider some motives to this glorious duty.

Failure to Give God Our Spirits in Worship Is a Very Great Sin

This sin of omission is the height of mockery and insult. To pay little or no attention to someone is a great offence. How much more does it offend God! To Israel God said, "Try treating your governor the way you treat me!" (See Mal. 1:8.) Failing to worship God in spirit is a sin against His majesty. It is like a man whose prince is speaking with him, who turns his back and begins to pet a dog. It is like a man who is guilty of treason who, instead of begging for pardon, sends his petition scribbled, torn, and smeared with excrement. Furthermore, failing to worship God in spirit is a sin against the very life of God, treating Him as if He were a deaf, dumb idol. It is a sin against the infinity of God, as if He were unworthy of our best. It is a sin against the spirituality of God, as if He were not a rational being. It is a sin against the supremacy of God, for it makes some other object the sovereign in our affections. It is a sin against the wisdom of God, putting earthly things above spiritual things, thus inverting the proper order. Imagining that God does not see our deepest thoughts, and that we can deceive Him with an outward show, like a whited sepulcher, is a sin against the omniscience of God. It is a sin against the holiness of God, as Proverbs 21:27 expresses: "The sacrifice of the wicked is abomination: how much more, when he bringeth it with a wicked mind?" It is a sin against the love of God, for it is a failure to reciprocate that love, like a debtor who mocks the kindness of his creditor by bringing him an empty purse instead of the payment. Finally, it is a sin against the sufficiency of God, declaring in effect that He does not satisfy us, and that we have found something more fulfilling to our hearts than Him. Instead of panting after Him like the deer after the water brooks, we instead find mud puddles more suitable to our taste.

The More Carnal Our Affections in Worship, the Clearer the Evidence That We Are in a Sinful State

Being easily satisfied with formalities in worship betrays a heart void of real love for God. Rather, it reveals a heart ready and willing to be diverted by the first paramour who comes along. O the hypocrisy of saying we love God, while living in such a state!

Carnal Worship Is a Grave Danger

We forfeit true comfort, which is found only in true worship. Think of the encouragement that John received on the isle of Patmos while he "was in the spirit on the Lord's day" (Rev. 1:10). But unspiritual worship is not only unacceptable to God but becomes an abomination to Him. He hates it.

In order to encourage spiritual worship, let us endeavor to maintain a spiritual frame of mind even when we are not actually worshiping. A careless weekday makes for a careless Sunday. Our sacrifice should burn continually. We must give no place to the devil.

Let us excite and exercise fervent love to God and dependence on Him.

Let us feed our minds with right and lofty thoughts of God. Remember who He is. He is unlike any earthly judge, for He judges the heart and not just the actions. The fear of God makes our worship serious; the joy of God makes our worship lasting.

Let us clear our hearts of inordinate desires after the world. These will choke the Word and make it unprofitable to us. As gravity keeps us from the sky, so a worldly mind keeps us from elevated worship. It is hard to meditate in the midst of a hurry of worldly affairs.

Let us be conscious of our spiritual needs, and how they can only be supplied in true worship. Stir up the same affections now that you should have on your deathbed.

Let us cast out any intruder who would spoil our worship. Even though it be something legitimate in itself, cut it up and root it out if it cumbers the ground of your soul.

Let us take advantage of every occasion in which God melts our heart and draws near in an extraordinary fashion. Be sensitive to His occasional special calls inviting you to commune with Him. More can be achieved by one strike on a hot iron than a hundred on a cold one.

Let us examine ourselves after every act of worship, to determine what hindered or impeded us. Then let us apply the blood of Christ by faith for our cure.

5

THE ETERNITY OF GOD

God is eternal in duration. In Psalm 90:2, Moses expresses this truth by saying, "Before the mountains were brought forth, or ever thou hadst formed the earth and the world, even from everlasting to everlasting, thou art God." This verse teaches us that the world had a beginning; that the world owes its existence to God, the Creator; that God existed before the world. Furthermore, we learn here that God alone is eternal; no other thing or person possesses the property of eternity. God exists in one permanent state, without succession. Obviously, this verse accommodates creatures of time by speaking as if eternity were divided into two parts, eternity past and eternity future, *from everlasting to everlasting*.

The whole concept of eternality is difficult for us to grasp. Time has beginning and ending. Eternity is contrary to time. It is an infinite immutable duration, without bounds. If God had a beginning, He might have an ending, and so would all our happiness, hope and being! The eternity of God is the foundation of the stability of all His covenant dealings with men.

Sometimes the words *eternal* and *everlasting* are used in Scripture with reference to things other than God. But these words must be understood to speak in a relative manner. Sometimes they describe something of a long duration that will have an end, such as the servant with his ear bored, who would be a servant forever (Deut. 15:17), even though the servitude would end at death. Other times, these terms describe that which has no end even though it had a beginning, such as the everlasting condition of angels and souls. They were nothing before they were something but will never be nothing again. However, when we speak of God's eternity, we speak of that which is unique to Him.

How God Is Eternal

Eternity is a negative concept. That is, we can better define what it is not than what it is. Such is true of many of the perfections of God, due to our creaturely limitations. To be eternal is not to be bound by time; it is a duration that knows no end. Now we will mark some respects in which eternity is God's attribute.

God has no beginning. God existed before the beginning, according to Genesis 1:1. It is impossible to designate a beginning point before time. Time began with the foundation of the world, but God was before time and therefore had no beginning. Outside of time there is only eternity. And nothing in eternity could have beginning; otherwise, it would not be eternal.

Everything with a beginning is dependent on that which gave it its being. God is independent. He depends on none for His beginning or being. He did not begin Himself, but rather He necessarily self-exists. This necessitates His being eternal.

God has no ending. "Thy years shall have no end," declares the Psalmist (102:27). As none gave Him His being, so none can deprive Him of it. There is no weakness in God that would introduce any corruption in Him. He alone is immortal by nature. "Who only hath immortality" (1 Tim. 6:16). All creatures who live forever depend on Him for their immortality; He could as easily annihilate us as create us. But none could annihilate God because He depends upon no one for His immortality.

There is no succession in God. The first part of the previous verse says, "Thou art the same." God not only remains in His being, but He remains the same in His being. How different from us! We change with time; something is added or lost every day. You are aging even as you read this page! Though some things remain the same for a season, yet there is constant motion, like a river that flows. But God is above time, and time has no effect on Him. There is no succession in His thoughts; He sees everything at once. Though there is succession and order in events as they are wrought in time, yet there is no succession with God in His knowledge of them. He has decreed their order but sees them all at once. In other words, there is no succession in the decrees of God, though there is succession in the execution of those decrees. God at once knows all and decrees all.

God is His own eternity. There is no concept of eternity apart from God. If there were no God, there would be no eternity existing separately, for all things, including eternity, are of God. Also, because He is eternal, all His perfections are likewise eternal. If anything necessary to His being ceased but for a moment, He could not be the eternal God.

God Must Be Eternal

We must humbly confess that we are over our heads here. There is no proportion between time and eternity. Nevertheless, the Word of God comes down to our level when speaking of eternity. Again, Psalm 102:27 states, "Thy years shall have no end." Even this verse accommodates our limited capacities by referring to something we can fathom, namely *years*. Of course, we should not literally assign years to the eternal One. Now we will mark some reasons why God must be eternal.

The very name by which He is known requires His eternity. The name Jehovah bears out His ever-presence. He told Moses that His name was "I Am That I Am" (Ex. 3:14). That is, His proper name indicates there is neither past nor future with Him. When we read of Him as who is and was and is to come (Rev. 1:8), we understand again that these terms better suit our weakness of thought rather than His greatness. He is an unbounded sea of being, an infinite life, an eternal present. There was never a point at which He was not what He now is, and what He is He will always be. His name will never be changed to *I Am Not!*

God has life in Himself (John 5:26). Life is essential to His essence. He gives life, but He receives no life. It is impossible that He should not live. His being is distinct from ours. "In Him we live and move and have our being" (Acts 17:28), but none gives Him His life, motion, and being. He alone necessarily exists; and what necessarily exists, exists from eternity.

God's immutability requires His eternity. If He had passed from a state of not being into a state of being, a dramatic change would have occurred. If He had moved from past to present, or if He moves from present to future, change would exist in Him. His eternity is a shield against all mutation. We will consider the immutability of God more in the next chapter.

God's infinite perfection requires His eternity. How could He be infinitely perfect and yet of finite duration? To be finite is the greatest of imperfection. But nothing can be added or subtracted from Him who is eternal.

God's almighty power requires His being eternal. Scripture links these two concepts together in Revelation 1:8, "I am Alpha and Omega, the beginning and the ending, saith the Lord, which is, and which was, and which is to come, the Almighty." If God came into being at some point, then His power also came into being, which means that there would have been a point at which there was no power with Him. Where there is no being, there is no power. Where there is no power, there is no omnipotence.

If God were not eternal, He would not be the first cause of all things. Only that which exists first has no beginning or ending. It exists necessarily of itself. The founder must exist before the foundation. If nothing existed from eternity, nothing exists now in time. If God is not the eternal Being, there could be no being now in time. Even a fool would not try to defend such silly notions! You must admit to an eternal Being, or else run into a hopeless maze of contradictions. Simply put, there must be an eternal, personal first cause.

God Alone Is Eternal

First Timothy 6:16 plainly says that the attribute of immortality is unique to God, "Who only hath immortality." This also indicates that the attribute of eternality is unique to God. The ongoing existence of creatures forever is not intrinsic to them; it is a donation from their Creator. Ours is a precarious life, forever dependent on the Giver of life, both here and hereafter. Any created thing cannot be eternal in the full sense of the word. What was once nothing cannot be eternal. What changed from being nothing to being something is mutable and therefore not eternal. No effect wrought by the will of a voluntary cause can be equal in duration to its cause. All created things are finite, which precludes being eternal, for eternity is infinite. Thus, eternity properly belongs to God alone.

What should we learn from this attribute?

Information

Christ is God. Eternity is attributed to the Son of God in Colossians 1:17, "He is before all things." The previous verse says, "By Him were all things created." Since eternity belongs only to God, and Christ is said to be eternal, then Christ is most certainly God. In the Old Testament, Melchizedek prefigured Christ's eternity in that he is said to have had "neither beginning of days, nor end of life, but made like unto the Son of God" (Heb. 7:3). Christ Himself speaks of the glory He had with the Father before the world was (John 17:5). The prophet Micah speaks of the coming Messiah as the One "whose goings forth have been from of old, from everlasting" (5:2). As the eternity of God is the ground of all religion, so the eternity of Christ is the ground of the Christian religion. His sufferings avail for our redemption because He suffered as the God-man. Only He could suffer like this.

All things are present to God. Eternity is one indivisible point, not divided into successive points, such as *before* and *after*. God does not depend on the passing of time to add to His knowledge. His knowledge is co-eternal with Him.

It is sinful folly to disagree with God and to question His decrees and actions. Eternity sets God apart from and above us. He alone sees the whole picture of time; we see only a small portion. As a baby possesses little understanding compared to a gray head, so much more are we, who are of so short a standing, beneath the wisdom of God. Since eternity cannot be comprehended in time, it should not be judged by a creature of time. Silence rather than censure becomes us when God's dealings are beyond our appreciation. Job was put to silence when God asked, "Where wast thou when I laid the foundations of the earth?" (Job 38:4). If we come to grips with our own smallness, we will reprove ourselves even for being overly curious concerning God's ways.

Every sin is an attack against the eternity of God. Every sin tends to destroy God, to reduce Him to a temporal being, treating Him as if He were contemptible like a mere creature. He that would put an end to God's glory by darkening it, would put an end to God's life by destroying it. All sin betrays a low evaluation of God in His perfections.

What a terror it is to lie under the condemnation of an eternal God! The thought of God's eternity is as dreadful to the God-hater as it is comforting to the God-lover. The criminal should tremble when he considers that the Judge and Executioner lives forever. The punishment of the lost will be proportionate to the greatness of their offenses and the glory of an eternal God.

Comfort

What good would any of His other perfections be without this one? If they were but temporary, we would have no lasting consolation.

Because God is eternal, His covenant is eternal. He confirmed His promise, swearing by Himself, that is, by His very life, which is an eternal life (Heb. 6:13). Before the foundation of the world, God promised eternal life to His people (Titus 1:2). This promise is good because He Himself is eternal in Himself. He holds eternity in His hand, and thus His covenant promises are steadfast and sure.

In covenant mercy, God becomes our God as an eternal possession. "This God is our God forever and ever" (Ps. 48:14). He is ours during this life, through death, in the resurrection, and throughout all the ages to come. The pleasures of God for His people are as unending as God Himself. Our happiness cannot perish as long as God lives.

The pleasures of God for His people are as durable as God Himself. They will never grow old, since they are not subject to the passing of time. In the glorified state, there will be no remorse over the past, and no anxiety for the future, as is often the case now, because the blessings of God will unceasingly flow. He may increase our delights, but He will not diminish them. This will be heaven—to enjoy an infinite and eternal God, who is not like a cistern that may run dry but like a fountain that continually springs.

In all our earthly distresses, the eternity of God should encourage us. Just as the revelation of I Am That I Am was given to strengthen Israel in their hour of need in Egypt, so the knowledge of this attribute should strengthen us. He is the great I Am to His people today. Our problems and persecutions are not eternal; they will certainly end. We need fear nothing that is merely temporal. Rather fear Him who alone is eternal.

We are furthermore comforted by considering that God's eternity makes His promises sure. "Trust in the Lord forever: for in the

Lord Jehovah is everlasting strength" (Isa. 26:4). Our trust in Him should match His eternity in its perpetuity. As God cannot die, so He cannot lie. "The word of our God shall stand forever" (Isa. 40:8). Man's best-made promises often fail because of unforeseen hindrances or even death. But God sees everything from the perspective of eternity, and death cannot touch Him. Though He may defer His promise a thousand years, yet is He "not slack concerning His promise," for He defers but a day (2 Peter 3:8–9). Who would not be willing to wait a day to receive an unspeakably delightful blessing?

Exhortation

We must repent of sins we committed long ago. The passing of time removes many sins from our memory, but with the eternal God they are ever-present. There is no statute of limitations in God's system of justice. If a thousand years is as one day with Him, then sins of twenty years ago are as if they had been committed within the last half-hour. Let us therefore be deeply grieved for our past, forgotten sins, which with God are still current issues.

We must be humbled before the eternal God. If we compare ourselves to lesser creatures, our feeling of greatness inflates, but compared to God, we are nothing. We cannot even fully conceive of God's eternity, let alone express it. Due to sin, we are more brutes than men in our understanding (Prov. 30:2). There is no proportion between time and eternity. God says, "I Am That I Am." But we must honestly say, "I am not what I am"—that is, "I do not self-exist; I exist only by an eternal sustaining power greater than I." Remember, we were made from the same material of which birds make their nests, in which worms dig, and upon which beasts tread. Our earthly existence is very, very brief. The terms of Scripture that speak of our life here include: a worm, grass, a flower, a vapor, and smoke. All these items quickly disappear. In God's sight, even the oldest man, Methuselah, lived less than a day! The angels who are as old as the earth tremble before God, and shall we who are but of yesterday strut with pride?

We must take our eyes off mere temporal, worldly things. Dare we prefer a momentary pleasure before an eternal God? What folly, to prefer a drop of dew to an ocean fullness! This whole earth is less than one week old in God's sight. What madness to allow our affections and confidence to rest in any earthly thing! Everything in this world is passing and perishing. "The fashion of this world passeth away," says the apostle (1 Cor. 7:31). Nothing here can satisfy us. We were made to commune with God, and nothing less can truly fill our hungry hearts. Those who live only for temporal things descend below their own nature and cease to be men. They will outlive this world and will fry in the flames of an everlasting, unquenchable fire.

We should think often and much on this attribute. This is one of the foundational articles of religion. "Now unto the King eternal, immortal, invisible, the only wise God, be honor and glory for ever and ever. Amen" (1 Tim. 1:17). What comfort would we find in any of God's perfections if He were subject to expire? On the other hand, what lasting pleasure can we expect to find in sin? Meditating on the eternity of God should keep sin from gaining a catch hold within us. Fleeting pleasures of sin appear ridiculous when cast into the balance of the eternity of God.

Finally, because God is eternal, He is worthy of our highest affections and deepest desires. We must see Him as worthy not only because of what He is to us, but especially because of what He is in Himself. Eternity is an awesome quality to possess. We creatures of time should marvel in the God of eternity. Also, we should gladly serve Him. Since God is eternal, He deserves our unending praise. Let us say with the psalmist, "I will sing unto the Lord as long as I live; I will sing praise to my God while I have my being" (104:33). The Ancient of Days has both eternal knowledge to remember our service to Him and eternal goodness to reward it.

6

THE IMMUTABILITY OF GOD

The most stable and unchangeable things we see are the heavenly bodies, including earth itself. These are the works of God's hands (Ps. 102:25). They are the best illustrations we have of God's immutability. But even these shall perish (v. 26). God who made them will change them. They will not be annihilated but refined, with improved qualities from those we now see. Pity the soul who lives only for that which will not endure! Perishing things cannot support our souls.

God is the same (v. 27). He never changes. His essence, nature, and perfections cannot be altered. Immutability signifies that nothing can be added or diminished. What God is, He always was. What He is, He always shall be. Eternity and immutability are linked together. Each implies the other. Immutability is the state itself; eternity is the measure of that state.

Considered in itself, immutability is not necessarily a perfection. The fallen angels are now unchangeable; but this constitutes their imperfection and misery. Immutability is a perfection in God because of His excellence of character. He is immutable in all His other attributes. So essential is immutability to Him that without it He could not be God.

Ways in Which God Is Immutable

God is immutable in His essence. God is the first being. His necessary self-existence proves His immutability. Since He derives

His being from no other, He cannot but be what He is. The fact that He is spirit and not body indicates that He is not subject to the physical changes that a composite being experiences. The fact that He is the only independent and eternal spirit indicates that He is unlike created spirits, who are capable of change.

If God were to change, it would have to be either for the better or for the worse. If for the better, then He is not now perfect and is not the infinite God. If for the worse, He would cease to be perfect. In either event, mutation would spoil His eternal perfection and true deity. Nor does God temporarily change from His original state and then revert to what He was. There is simply no change in Him at all.

God is immutable in His knowledge. God knows all, and He has always known all. He has never gained knowledge, for there is nothing more for Him to know. His knowledge is perfect and cannot change.

If God were mutable, He would not be an object worthy of our trust. He would not be a competent judge of anything, and truth would be impossible to pin down. Unlike man, whose knowledge is separate from himself and grows or diminishes, God's knowledge is an essential property of His. He knows all things by one intuitive act. As there is no succession in His being, so there is no succession in His knowledge. He comprehends all things at once, including what we call the *future*.

Furthermore, God's knowledge and will is the cause of all things, not the effect of these things. Thus, we read in Acts 15:18, "Known unto God are all his works from the beginning of the world." Our distinction of *past* and *future* implies no change in God's knowledge. Of course, He sees succession in things, but there is no succession in His knowledge of them. "His understanding is infinite" (Ps. 147:5). We are obviously out of our league here. God's immutable knowledge is incomprehensible to us!

God is immutable in His will and purpose. Any such change would imply some opposition to His previous plans and would make Him an enemy to Himself. The truth is, God's will is essential to His being; it is not a component added to His being. Otherwise, He would not be the simplest (uncompounded) being. There is perfect agreement between God's knowledge and His will. He knows all that exists, and the existence of anything presupposes an act of His will. Just as His knowledge is one intuitive act, so His will is one act of volition. Therefore, we often read in Scripture of the *counsel* of God, not *counsels* in the plural. For example, "The counsel of the Lord standeth forever" (Ps. 33:11). There is one perfect and unchangeable act of will in God.

There is no reason for God to change His will concerning anything. When a man changes his will, it is due to lack of foresight, lack of power, or instability. But God knows all, is almighty, and is unwavering. Though God and His decree are immutable, the things He decrees may be mutable according to His will. The subsequent change in the thing does not imply a change in God's decree.

"But liberty to change is the height of perfection," someone may argue. "Immutability infringes on God's freedom." But this is not sound reasoning. God is freely immutable; He does not wish to be other than He is. It is no mark of imperfection to be perfectly good. Rather it is the height of perfection to be unchangeable in perfection.

God is immutable in terms of place. He is present everywhere. If He were to move about from place to place, there would be change of location. However, He is ubiquitous or omnipresent. "Do not I fill heaven and earth? saith the Lord" (Jer. 23:24). It is inconceivable that any place could exist where God is not present. He who has no cause of being has no limits of being.

When God is said to come down to earth or to draw near to man, it is not by a change of place on God's part, but by the special influence of His Spirit. It is more His drawing us to Him rather than His coming to us. For example, we speak of the morning sun coming into our room, yet the sun has not really changed; rather, its rays penetrate our window. Or passengers on a boat say that land is drawing near when, in reality, it is they who are being drawn near to land by the man on the dock with the rope. God is an immovable rock; we are floating and uncertain creatures. He moves in us to change our minds, affections, and wills. He remains always the same.

Proof That God Is Immutable

The name *Jehovah* proves God's immutability. To be the I Am is not only to be eternal but also to be stable. God's name will never simply be I Was or I Shall Be.

God's perfection proves His immutability. If He changed for the better, then there would be some perfection outside and above Him. If He changed for the worse, there would be no perfection in Him, and He would be an enemy to His own glory. Does man in some way add to God's perfection? Only as much as the light of a candle adds to the sun! Is God's perfection sullied by the sin of man? Only as much as the light of the sun is darkened by an enemy shooting arrows against it!

God's simplicity proves His immutability. That which is composed of parts or pieces admits of change. One of the parts may be removed. But that which is simple cannot be divided, and thus cannot change. The first cause of all things must be simple, for if it were compound it would depend on its parts and could not be the first thing. In other words, there is nothing in God which is not God.

God's eternity proves His immutability. All change resembles death: something ceases to be. But since God is before time, He cannot be changed by time. With Him there is no new essence, nor knowledge nor purpose. If God were to change at all, there is no reason why He might eventually cease to exist altogether, for all changeableness implies corruptibility.

God's infinity and power proves His immutability. All change implies limits and bounds. If anything were added to Him, He would not be infinite to begin with. If anything were diminished from Him, He would no longer be infinite. Likewise with His almighty power—to add to it or subtract from it is impossible.

God's governing of creation proves His immutability. All things are moved by a power that is stable. Otherwise, there would be no order in the motions of the universe. All would be chaos. God is the orderer and governor of all motion and must of necessity be immutable.

Only God Is Immutable

Mutability is inherent in every creature. Our very coming into existence was a tremendous change from nothing to something. In the first chapter of Hebrews, one argument for the deity of Christ hinges on the fact that all creation changes. "They shall be changed: but thou art the same" (v. 12). No created thing can be absolutely perfect; all depend on God, and all admit room for greater perfection. This applies to creation before Adam's fall as well as after.

All corporeal creation is subject to change. Even the sun, which has been in its place since creation and appears so constant, has changed. It stood still in Joshua's time and moved backward in Hezekiah's time, at the will of God. Man, the noblest of God's creatures, is subject to change. Think of how many changes just one day can bring to us!

All spiritual creation is subject to change. The angels increase in knowledge, and their worship of God increases accordingly. "To the intent that now unto the principalities and powers in heavenly places might be known by the church the manifold wisdom of God" (Eph. 3:10).

Arguments Against God's Immutability Answered

Did not God change when He created the world? Creation involved great changes indeed, but not on the part of God. There was no new will in God when He created, for His determination to create was from eternity. The work was new, but the decree was purposed in Himself before the foundation of the world. He executes nothing in time which He has not ordained from eternity. Imagine a builder who has fixed in his mind what he will build, even though he may not build it for many years. His beginning to build does not involve a change in his will at the time of building; he simply is carrying out what he planned before. So with God, except that His will is eternally in Himself.

Furthermore, there was no new power with God when he began to create. His power was His from eternity, though He manifested it in the work of creation.

Nor was there any new relation acquired by God in creation. Since He eternally possessed the prerogatives of creating even without creating, He can rightly be called the Creator from eternity. The act of creating was no change in His essence, knowledge or will.

Did not God change in the incarnation of the Son? No, there was no change whatsoever in the nature of the Son when He assumed human nature. He took the form of a servant but did not lose the form of God. His essential glory was not changed, but simply veiled from human sight. Both the divine and human natures preserved their peculiar properties. Obviously, His human nature was subject to change. Yet throughout His earthly life, and even in His sufferings on the cross, He did not cease to be God.

Does not God change when He repents (as the Scriptures sometimes say)? Not in the same sense in which repentance applies to man. To us, repentance is necessary because of a mistake or for lack of foresight. But God makes no mistakes, and there are no unexpected turns of events with Him. So also with His grieving. God is not subject to passions as we know them. He is "blessed [i.e., happy] for ever" (Rom. 9:5). However, in His Holy Word, God often accommodates Himself to our weak capacity of understanding. He condescends to speak to us like a man. He informs us by our own phrases, like a nurse who talks in broken language to young children. Were it not so, how little of Him would we perceive!

Repentance in God has only to do with His dealings with man. When He repented that He had made man on the earth (Gen. 6:5), there was a change in God's outward conduct from a way of kindness to a way of severity. But there was no change in His eternal, immutable counsel and will. Such repentings are according to what God decreed from eternity.

Does not God change when He does not carry out His threats? The threats issued by God are warnings against sinners, showing God's right to punish them for their sin. But these threats are conditional: they declare what God will do if man continues unrepentant in sin. They do not declare what God has absolutely decreed from eternity. When a threat is not carried out by God, it is not due to any change in Him, but rather to a change on the part of the sinner. So likewise with God's promises to bless: they assume perseverance in well doing on the part of God's people. These conditions are not always expressed, for they need not be. The Ninevites understood that although God had, through the preaching of Jonah, promised judgment, yet He might spare them if they repented. When God told Hezekiah to prepare to die, he was driven to prayer and increased humiliation. To threaten when sins are high is a part of God's justice; not to execute when sins are revoked by repentance is a part of God's goodness. Through these means He accomplishes His immutable will.

Does not God change when He is angry with one He loves or is appeased where He has been angry? The answer is the same as with the previous question. It is the creature that changes, not God. His holiness is constant; moral creatures change with relation to

His holiness. Is the sun changed when it hardens one object and softens another? Or when it makes a flower more fragrant and a dead carcass fouler?

In redemption, Christ reconciled God to man, but not by altering God's will in any way. It was the will of the Father that the Son should come to redeem in the first place. Christ did not change the Father's will; He carried it out. He said, "Lo, I come . . . to do thy will, O God" (Heb. 10:7).

Did not God change when the Old Testament economy gave way to the New Testament? A physician does not prescribe the same medicine to every patient. Yet his will and skill remain the same. It is the capacity and need of the patients that vary. Even so, God determined what was preparatory and what would follow. He did not change in bringing the old covenant to an end, any more than He changed in establishing it to begin with. There was no change in the divine will, only in the execution of the divine will.

Now let us consider what we should learn.

Information

Since God alone is immutable, Christ is God. The Scriptures give abundant testimony to the unchanging nature of the second person of the Trinity. For example, Hebrews 1 quotes from Psalm 45, speaking prophetically of Christ, "Thy throne, O God, is for ever and ever" (v. 8). Then it quotes from Psalm 102, referring to the change that Christ will bring upon creation (v. 12). Yet the Changer remains unchanged.

It is not in vain to serve God. How could we worship a God who changed colors like a chameleon? Nothing would be definite with Him. He might become an unrighteous God tomorrow. We would only be guessing as to who He is or whether His revealed will remained in effect. How could we even pray to such an unpredictable God? When we pray, we acknowledge our dependence on Him.

But we could not depend on a changing God. Remember, we do not pray to change Him but to ask Him for what He has already purposed to give.

Mankind is vastly different from God. There was every reason for our utter humility before the fall; how much more afterward! The only unchangeable thing about us is our changeability. We are unstable in our knowledge; we oppose the truth and are naturally blown about by every wind of doctrine. We are unstable in our affections and will; like Israel, we halt between two opinions. Even believers are variable; like Peter we vow to follow, then deny. We are unstable in our actions, like Nebuchadnezzar who praised the God of Daniel, but soon built a huge idol. Even Paul had reason to mourn, "When I would do good, evil is present with me" (Rom. 7:21).

The ungodly should take heed. God will not change His nature and law so that sinners might remain unchanged in their sin. He will never approve of sin. Peace with this immutable God requires change on the sinner's part, turning away from sin.

Comfort

If ever there was a reason to trust God, then there is reason now. God is as ready now as ever He was to receive any who come to Him. He is as worthy of our trust now as ever He was. His covenant of grace remains unchanged. It does not state, "I will be their God if they will be my people," but rather, "[I] will be their God, and they shall be my people" (Jer. 31:33). In a sense, He puts a condition of faith on His covenant, yet He imparts that faith in the hearts of His elect. Then He continues to work mightily in us that we might persevere in that faith. He writes His law in our hearts. We depend entirely upon the power of His grace to keep us from forsaking Him. His immutability further assures our eternal happiness in heaven. We will receive a kingdom that, like its King, cannot be moved (Heb. 12:28).

Exhortation

Let us not settle on this world. It is ever-changing. All is subject to decay. Lot chose the fertile plain, but it soon became brimstone. We all naturally desire something steady and sure, but we will never find it on this earth. Do not waste much time or thought upon temporal things. What folly to neglect the immutable God for mutable earth! Do not trust in nor rejoice in temporal things. Wealth, honor, and even knowledge can quickly fail. All God's temporal benefits are revocable. How much better to enjoy the Benefactor Himself, who cannot change! Any other enjoyment is but for a moment. We must prefer God above all other things.

Let us be patient under all God's providences. The rectitude of our wills consists in conformity to God's will. To be discontent is to contend with Him. He is immutably good to us, even when He corrects us. Since He is for us, nothing can be against us, least of all Himself. The more clearly He makes His will known to us, the more sinful is our struggling against it. What arrogance for us to want God to change His purpose and nature so that we might not have to suffer any changes!

Let us imitate God's perfection by endeavoring to be immutable in holiness. "Therefore, my beloved brethren, be ye stedfast, unmoveable" (1 Cor. 15:58). "Let us hold fast the profession of our faith without wavering" (Heb. 10:23). God is constant in His promises, and so ought we to be in our obedience. God delights in seeing His people resemble Him as much as we can. To be more like Him, we must draw nearer to Him.

7

THE OMNIPRESENCE OF GOD

In the days of the prophet Jeremiah, false prophets abounded who promised peace and safety. They spoke as if God knew nothing of the national sins of Judah. God challenges their error by asking in chapter 23, verse 24, "Can any hide himself in secret places that I shall not see him? saith the LORD. Do not I fill heaven and earth? saith the LORD." God argues for his knowledge of all their deeds on the basis of His being present everywhere. Not only does His power and authority fill all heaven and earth but His very essence fills every place. There is no place without Him.

If God exists, He must be somewhere. According to Scripture, He is everywhere. As He is not limited by time, He is not limited by space. However, man's natural thinking often limits God to some place, such as the Jewish temple, or the hills but not the valleys (1 Kings 20:23). To correct our thinking, we will first consider some basic propositions concerning God's omnipresence.

General Propositions

Proposition 1. We must understand what this attribute is not. God is not bound by space, as we are. His nature knows no bounds. When He is said to be present in one place, He is not absent from another place. As no place can exist without God, so no place can contain Him.

Proposition 2. There is an influential omnipresence of God. Simply by virtue of being the Creator, God is everywhere. Nothing would continue without His providential sustaining. The continuation of anything implies that He is present with it.

Of course, He is present in more specific ways. He is present with every creature as it fulfills its purpose with the capacity He gives it. He is near to rational creatures, endowed with a soul. There is His gracious presence with His redeemed people. He is present with His churches. He is even present in hell to torment the damned. In many ways it can be said that He fills heaven and earth.

Proposition 3. There is an essential omnipresence of God. Since He gives all creation to have its place, He must be in each place, for He cannot give what He does not have.

As all time is but a moment to God's eternity, so all places are as but a point to His essence. He is both larger than time and vaster than space. Many people have an idea of God's presence which renders Him little more than a living statue, moved about from place to place. But the psalmist corrects our thinking when he asks, "Whither shall I go from thy spirit? or whither shall I flee from thy presence? If I ascend up into heaven, thou art there: if I make my bed in hell, behold, thou art there. If I take the wings of the morning, and dwell in the uttermost parts of the sea; Even there shall thy hand lead me, and thy right hand shall hold me" (Ps. 139:7–10).

If God is in all places, it follows that He is with all creatures who inhabit any of those places. "He be not far from every one of us: for in him we live, and move, and have our being" (Acts 17:27–28). In some sense, the Divine essence is equally present with all creatures in heaven, earth, and hell. Of course, this presence is not His gracious saving presence, which is limited according to His will. In the more general sense, we might say that the world is in Him more than He is in the world. The Creator contains the world, but the world contains not the Creator.

We should understand that the omnipresence of God does not imply that He mixes with creation, as if His essence were changed. Nor does He divide, so that He is part in heaven and part on earth. The simplicity of His nature allows no division. Nor does He multiply Himself in order to be present everywhere, since an infinite being cannot be enlarged. Nor is His essence spread thin, like beaten gold, to cover every place. Rather, He is simply totally present, as much in one place as another.

Proposition 4. God is present beyond the world. The universe itself does not limit His omnipresence; He is not confined to creation. As He is larger than time, so He is larger than space. In 1 Kings 8:27 Solomon prayed, "But will God indeed dwell on the earth? behold, the heaven and heaven of heavens cannot contain thee; how much less this house that I have builded?" God can no more be contained in one place since creation than before creation.

Proposition 5. Omnipresence is a quality unique to God and incommunicable to any created thing. Otherwise, the omnipresent creature would be equal to God, which is both unscriptural and impossible. Not even the human nature of the God-man, the Lord Jesus Christ, is omnipresent.

Proofs of God's Omnipresence

First, God's infinity proves His omnipresence. He has no bounds, and He has no parts, therefore He must be totally present everywhere. All God's perfections are infinite: "His greatness is unsearchable" (Ps. 145:3). He could not be infinite in all aspects except for His presence, for that would spoil every other perfection. We might as well speak of confining His power and wisdom as to speak of confining His presence.

Second, God's continuing operations in the world prove His omnipresence. He providentially preserves His creation. If He were to withdraw Himself, all things would cease to live, move and have being. Even the second causes, through which He often operates, depend upon Him.

Third, God's supreme perfection proves His omnipresence. In the same way in which that which has life is more perfect than that which has no life, so that which is present everywhere is more perfect than that which is limited to only one place. Omnipresence is perfection of location. There is no power above God to restrain Him to a certain place. Nor can He restrain Himself from any place, for that would amount to denying Himself of His own perfection.

Mankind was made in the image and likeness of God. When we see any excellence in man, it is but a token of a perfection that is eminently in God. Psalm 94:9 asks, "He that planted the ear, shall he not hear? he that formed the eye, shall he not see?" Thus, inasmuch as it is an excellence for man to occupy one place, it is supreme perfection for God to occupy every place.

Fourth, God's immutability proves His omnipresence. If He moved about from place to place, His location would change. But God cannot change, as we have already considered.

Fifth, God's omnipotence proves His omnipresence. If God so desired, He could create a million worlds. He has the power to do that. And His power is not greater than His essence. As we can conceive of no limit to His power, so we can conceive of no limit to His presence. Inasmuch as He created all places, He fills all places. He did not create any place where He is now shut out.

Objections Answered

Is not this doctrine weakened by the statements in Scripture where God is said to dwell in heaven and in the temple? None of these passages say He dwells only in those places. Heaven is the court of His majestic presence but not the prison of His essence. There He reigns without any opposition to His government. There He makes the greatest discoveries of Himself to rational creation. From there His blessings descend to earth. He dwells in heaven in regard to the expression of His glory; He dwells in hell in regard to the expression of His justice; He dwells in earth by the display of His wisdom, power and patience; He dwells in His people as monuments of His grace; He dwells in all in regard to His substance.

The Old Testament further speaks of God's dwelling in the temple and in the ark of the covenant. But He could only dwell both in heaven and on earth if He is omnipresent. In each instance, it was the same essence, though different manifestations.

Is not this doctrine impaired by the statements in Scripture where God is said to come to us or depart from us? Rather than being understood to speak of His essential presence, these statements refer to some special manifestation of Himself. Such manifestations include coming in saving grace or in comforting presence, assisting providence, or in direction and protection. Or He may depart in terms of certain special manifestations, such as the withdrawing of mercy and coming in judgment.

Is not this doctrine disparaged by God's being present with the lowest forms of creation? Since it was not beneath His dignity to create them, it is not beneath His dignity to fill them. Otherwise, He could never have created them at all. Everything He made was "very good" (Gen. 1:31). If God were to create anything of which He would later become ashamed, He would diminish His own character by creating it, and thereby impugn His own wisdom.

If God fills all things, then are not all things God? No, the doctrine is not that God is everywhere by means of conjunction, composition or mixture. As the sun shines on objects but does not become one with those objects, so God is not mixed with what He touches. If everything were God, then He would lose His distinct character, and nothing but God would exist; He could inhabit nothing, for as soon as He created it, it would be God. However, the infinite and the finite cannot be so joined. Even in the incarnation of the Second Person of the godhead, the divine and human natures remain distinct. As fish live and move in the water, but are not water, and as we live and move in air, but are not air, so God is everywhere, but remains distinct from everywhere.

If God is everywhere, can we not worship any of His creation and not be guilty of idolatry? This argument has been used to justify idolatry, and some who argued against it have done so by denying the omnipresence of God altogether. But the right answer is the same as we said above: the nature of created objects remains distinct from the nature of the Creator who fills them all. To admit idolatry on this basis is like honoring the servant who escorts the prince rather than the prince himself. It is nothing but treason.

Is not God defiled by being present with defiled objects? If it were so, then His power would be defiled for having created them at all, for all objects are His, whether in their created or fallen states. Defilement cannot attach to God. Is a man's spirit defiled by the diseased body in which it dwells? Are the sunbeams defiled by shining on a dunghill? Again, there is no mixture of God's nature with the nature of that which He fills.

What should learn much from this attribute?

Information

Christ has a divine nature. He is more than a mere man. He said to Nicodemus, "No man hath ascended up to heaven, but he that came down from heaven, even the Son of man which is in heaven" (John 3:13). Note that He speaks in the present tense. Even while He was on earth in His human nature speaking to Nicodemus, He was nonetheless in heaven with regard to His divine nature. John 1:10 says, "He was in the world, and the world was made by him." He was in the world as God before He was in world as man. Moreover, He promised to be present with His people unto the end of the age (Matt. 28:20). This is only possible because He is omnipresent and is therefore God.

This attribute agrees with God's spiritual mode of existence. If the omnipresent God existed with a physical body, there would be no place left for anything or anyone else. But as a spirit, God penetrates all and acts in all.

This attribute argues for divine providence. If God is everywhere, then He is concerned with everything. It is inconceivable that His presence should be to no purpose.

This attribute argues for God's omniscience. Because He is an intelligent Being, and is everywhere present, He of necessity must know everything. Consider again Jeremiah 23:24, "Can any hide himself in secret places that I shall not see him? saith the LORD." God's patience with sinners is not due to any ignorance on His part concerning their sin. He sees all sin up close and cannot but see it.

This attribute argues the incomprehensibility of God. Nothing is more present than God, yet nothing is more hidden. He comprehends us, but we do not comprehend Him. He is known by faith, enjoyed by love, but comprehended by no mind. Only He fully knows Himself.

God is wonderful and great, but we are nothing. There is a vast disproportion between God and creation. We are limited, finite, impure, weak, foolish, and small. What little, little, little things we are to God! Angels hide their faces from Him—how much more ought creeping worms like us humble ourselves before Him! When a man gets a first glimpse of the ocean, he is taken back with its vastness. Likewise, we should be swallowed up in admiration at the thought of the immensity of God.

This attribute is often forgotten or held in contempt. Here again is atheism, practically speaking: many people live as if God were present nowhere. How quickly did Adam lose sight of God's omnipresence, hoping to escape from God's view behind some trees! Further, how many good men forget God when they begin to fear any creature, when God's Word to us is, "Fear not, for I am with thee" (Isa. 43:5).

How many today hold this attribute in contempt by committing in the presence of God what they would be afraid or ashamed to do before the eyes of men! How many a man is kept from theft by the presence of other men. This simply betrays a greater fear of man than of God, who is present at all times. It is a debasing of God in the heart and is a very great evil. It is like a wife who commits adultery before her husband's face. "Ye did evil before mine eyes" (Isa. 65:12). David sinned secretly, but later cried out to God, "Against thee, thee only, have I sinned, and done this evil in thy sight" (Ps. 51:4). This consideration should especially sting our hearts with deep conviction for all our sins.

This attribute should strike terror in the hearts of the lost. There is no hiding from God. No deed can be hidden, nor even the desire that never develops into a deed. "The eyes of the LORD are in every place, beholding the evil and the good" (Prov. 15:3).

Comfort

This truth is as much a comfort to a godly man as it is a terror to a wicked man.

In times of violent temptation, God does not desert us. When Satan hurls a fiery dart, God is with us as well as with the archer! God is closer to us than our closest enemy. To prevail against us, our enemies must remove God from us. In other words, they would have to cause Him to cease to be God altogether, and this can never be. They will ultimately be put to shame. "There were they in great fear: for God is in the generation of the righteous" (Ps. 14:5).

In times of sharp affliction, God is near. "When thou passest through the waters, I will be with thee" (Isa. 43:2). He is a sanctuary to His people in all their adversities. "God is our refuge and strength, a very present help in trouble" (Ps. 46:1). Consider the testimony of Paul, the persecuted apostle: "At my first answer no man stood with me, but all men forsook me. . . . Notwithstanding the Lord stood with me, and strengthened me" (2 Tim. 4:16–17).

In all our duties of worship, God is near, not only essentially, but also in a special and gracious way. Whether we meet in a palace or in a cave, God is there. Though we bow in our closet to pray, He is there.

In any difficult task or calling, God's presence comforts us. Moses was sent on a difficult errand, but God promised, "I will be with thy mouth, and teach thee what thou shalt say" (Ex. 4:12). God's assistance encourages His servants laboring under unpromising conditions.

This divine presence means that the resources of all God's perfections are with us at all times, for He is simple and undivided. Everywhere we have His wisdom to guide us, His power to support us, His mercy to pity us, His goodness to relieve us. This should rejoice our hearts greatly.

Exhortation

Let us meditate much on this truth. This attribute makes all the others sweet to our souls. What good would God's grace, wisdom, and power be to us from a distance? We must, like David, "set the Lord always before me" (Ps. 16:8). If we do not, our personal religion will grow feeble. The verse concludes, "Because he is at my right hand, I shall not be moved." Remembering this truth will instill a deep fear of God in our hearts.

This truth will be a shield against temptations. One look from Christ brought Peter to his senses. What man would be so stupid as to rob a house while the judge is watching?

It will spur us on to holy conduct. Jacob was thus moved: "Surely the LORD is in this place; and I knew it not. . . . How dreadful is this place!" (Gen. 28:16–17).

It will subdue distractions in the worship of God. When the teacher is present, the students mind their books. When the master is watching, the servant cannot be idle. Let us earnestly seek a sense of God's special presence. Let us not be content with the same presence of God that brutes and devils have. We need His gracious presence to confer true happiness upon us. This will enable us to enjoy a heaven upon earth.

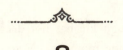

8

THE KNOWLEDGE OF GOD

Nothing so delights a gracious soul as an opportunity to praise the perfections and goodness of God. He both deserves and demands our worship. It is our privilege and duty. Psalm 147:5 says, "Great is our Lord, and of great power: his understanding is infinite." Notice that this verse links God's power and knowledge. All His perfections are infinite. In the previous chapter we dealt with His presence, which is likewise closely tied with His knowledge, which we will now consider.

This attribute needs no proving. All men instinctively know something of it. Even pagans demonstrate their consciousness of God's knowledge by offering their vain repetitions and sacrifices to gods whom they assume are watching.

That Kind of Knowledge That Is in God

This quality is known by various names, such as God's remembrance, sight, foreknowledge (or prescience, in this sense), omniscience, knowledge, wisdom and prudence. Regardless of what we call it, we must remember not to measure His understanding by our own. As the heavens are higher than the earth, so are His thoughts higher than our thoughts (Isa. 55:9).

There are various ways to divide this knowledge. For example, we may distinguish between knowledge of vision and knowledge of intelligence. By the former, God knows all that has been, is, and shall be, because He has decreed it so. By the latter, God knows all possibilities, even though He has not decreed to do them. After all, He could have made more worlds and more people, had He desired. Or we may divide knowledge into the speculative, which is known without any working or operation, and the practical, which involves working to exhibit the knowledge. Again, there is knowledge of approbation and of apprehension. This distinction in clearly made in Scripture. God's love and approval are spoken of in terms of knowledge. He said to Israel, "You only have I known of all the families of the earth" (Amos 3:2). On judgment day He will declare to the lost, "I never knew you: depart from me, ye that work iniquity" (Matt. 7:23). Though God knows the lost so as to understand them, He does not know them so as to savingly love them.

That Which God Knows

He knows Himself. He alone has this knowledge. No created being fully understands itself. But the Creator, who is infinite in perfection, possesses infinite knowledge by which to have perfect and comprehensive self-knowledge. "The things of God knoweth no man, but the Spirit of God" (1 Cor. 2:11). Even the angels who surround and serve Him have an imperfect knowledge of Him. If God's self-knowledge were imperfect, He would be ignorant of the most excellent object. He would not be able to govern since He would not know His own power. Nor could He punish because He would not know what constituted an attack against Himself. Truly, He could not know other things if He knew not Himself.

He knows all things that are to be known. His knowledge is without bounds. If there were anything He did not know, He would not be God.

First, He knows all that which never shall be. That is, He knows that which exists only in the realm of possibility. For example, He knew that the inhabitants of Keilah would deliver David into Saul's hand if he remained there (1 Sam. 23:11). Christ knew what means would have brought Tyre and Sidon to repent had they been brought to bear upon the inhabitants of those cities (Matt. 11:21). In some measure, even man possesses some knowledge of possibility. We weigh various schemes and outcomes when making decisions. How much more does the omniscient God know all that which could be! He did not exhaust His knowledge in creation. All things are possible with Him. From this infinite realm of possibility, He has appointed by an act of His will what actually shall occur. How absurd to imagine that He gathered information from the creatures while drawing up His plan! Perfect knowledge was at His disposal. Thus, there are unlimited possibilities known in His power, though not known in His will. This is a deep and humbling consideration and is cause for admiration of the omniscient God.

Second, God also knows all that which to us is past. He delights in His perfect knowledge of past things, as opposed to the ignorance of false gods: "Let them show the former things, what they be, that we may consider them, and know the latter end of them" (Isa. 41:22). Our capacity to remember things is but a reflection of God's perfect knowledge. With Him, it is as if the past is still present. When we read in the Scripture of God's not remembering sins, we understand it is a judicial forgetfulness; He will not bring them up again. On the other hand, when we read of His remembering His word or covenant, it indicates His fulfilling of His promise.

Third, God knows all things present. If He did not, then man and even beast could boast of greater knowledge than God. "But all things are naked and opened unto the eyes of him with whom we have to do" (Heb. 4:13). He knows all the stars and all the sparrows and every cloud and every snowflake. If God failed to know even a fly, He would not be God. He knows all the actions of all creatures. The words that the king of Syria uttered in his bedroom were revealed by God to Elisha (2 Kings 6:12). God knows all the thoughts of rational creatures, whether good or evil. "Thou understandest my thoughts afar off" (Ps. 139:2). If it were not so, the tenth commandment, "Thou shalt not covet," would be impossible to enforce, as well as the first and great commandment; thus, God might be deceived. But on the day of judgment, He "will make manifest the counsels of the hearts" (1 Cor. 4:5). In fact, God alone is able to fully know any heart. "The heart is deceitful above all things, and desperately wicked: who can know it? I the LORD search the heart, I try the reins, even to give every man according to his ways, and according to the fruit of his doings" (Jer. 17:9–10). God does not acquire new knowledge of the heart by watching it in action because this would make Him dependent on the creature. God learned nothing new when He said to Abraham on Mount Moriah, "Now I know that thou fearest God." Rather, Abraham's fear of God had been publicly manifested. Previously God had said, "For I know him, that he will command his children and his household after him, and they shall keep the way of the LORD" (Gen. 22:12; 18:19). Finally, God knows all the sins of creatures. If He did not know evil, how could He permit it, order it, punish it, or pardon it? By knowing Himself, He knows all that is contrary to Himself, yet He is not defiled thereby.

Fourth, God knows all things future. If He did not possess this knowledge, there could be no providence at all. If the future inclinations and actions of Potiphar and Pharaoh were unknown to God, then the sending of Joseph into Egypt might have proved a terrible blunder on God's part. Moreover, from our perspective, there was a point at which everything in time was future with God. Dare we say that He did not then know all things future? He has given abundant proof of this knowledge of the future in the prophecies of Scripture, every one of which He fulfills. In Isaiah 41:23, God lays down this challenge to man: "Show the things that are to come hereafter, that we may know that ye are gods." Of course, man has some little knowledge of future events. For example, by careful calculation he can predict a solar eclipse. This is but a reflection of the perfect knowledge in God. The only things that are in the future are those things He has decreed to be in the future, and He knows His own decrees. "Known unto God are all his works from the beginning of the world" (Acts 15:18). God's knowledge does not arise from things because they exist, but because He wills them to exist. Otherwise, creatures would have a cause apart from Him, and He would be indebted to them for His knowledge. He knows what will be, because it cannot be without His will. God's knowledge is immutable; it is not subject to the changes of having new information or people or circumstances added with the passing of time. God's knowledge of possible things runs parallel with His power, and His knowledge of future things runs parallel with His will. Oftentimes future events were recorded in Scripture in terms of the past or present: "For unto us a child is born, unto us a son is given" (Isa. 9:6). "Surely he hath borne our griefs, and carried our sorrows" (Isa. 53:4). Only God can speak with certainty on the future, as if it were present or already past. Satan pretended to know the future when he said concerning Job, "Put forth thine hand now, and touch all that he hath, and he will curse thee to thy face" (1:11). All we know for sure about the future is what God has revealed to us about it. Though we cannot comprehend how God knows all things future, we must nevertheless believe that it is so. Our knowledge is not the measure of His knowledge. How foolish for us to admit only what we can perfectly conceive of Him!

Fifth, God knows all future contingencies, sometimes called accidents or chance. The arrow that struck Ahab appeared as a mere haphazard act on the part of the unpredictable free will of a soldier. But it was no surprise to God. Arrogant man would like to make God just as ignorant of contingencies as himself; he prefers a God who can be deceived by the sudden, unexpected changes in the will of man, a God who depends on man for information. Such a God cannot truly govern the world. He would be a perplexed God, who waits to see what man will do before He can act. But the truth is, God knows all the free and voluntary acts of man beforehand. "There are many devices in a man's heart; nevertheless the counsel of the LORD, that shall stand" (Prov. 19:21). Nothing is more voluntary than parents naming their children, yet God prophesied of the coming of Cyrus hundreds of years before his birth (Isa. 44:28). Therefore, his name could be nothing but Cyrus! We could cite many similar examples from Scripture. Perhaps the greatest is the crucifixion of Christ. The Jewish leaders were vehement in their demands for it. It was their will. Yet, their actions were all determined beforehand. "Him, being delivered by the determinate counsel and foreknowledge of God, ye have taken, and by wicked hands have crucified and slain," preached Peter in Acts 2:23. This was the "eternal purpose" of God (Eph. 3:11). It necessitated the fall of Adam and the occasion for redemption. God knew exactly how Satan would tempt, as well as where Adam would be weakest. God withheld the restraint that would have empowered Adam to resist the temptation. In all the actions of mankind, God knows how much grace He will bestow, and how much He will withhold, and what actions of good or evil will eventuate. Furthermore, He does not depend on the will of man to know what man's voluntary actions will be. This is a deep subject, but at least this much must be said.

Now, let us consider six principles as a summary with respect to God's knowledge and man's will.

1. The fact that something must occur does not take away the liberty of the doer. We may act freely, even though God determined our actions beforehand.

2. Will cannot be compelled, for then it would cease to be will. When we have done what we desired, we cannot honestly say that anything was forced on us. Adam dared not accuse God of forcing him to sin. Judas, who heard Christ foretell of the betrayal, dared not accuse Christ of causing his sin; he acted freely, and became filled with feelings of unbearable personal guilt.

3. Considered in itself, God's prescience is not the cause of anything. Even man with his limited foreknowledge of things does not thereby cause them to be. I may know that if a drunkard enters a bar, he will become drunk, but my knowledge of the fact is not causative to it. God's foreknowledge does not take away the liberty of man's will.

4. God foreknows things because they will come to pass, but they do not come to pass because He knows them. Some things God has willed to do Himself. Other things He has willed to permit His creatures to do by withholding His restraint from them. (This clears God from any complicity in sin or authorship of it.)

5. God not only foreknew the actions of man, but also the will of man. God's knowledge of man does not cause man to become less than man. Though God knows free agents, yet they remain in a position of freedom, not compulsion. In other words, Gods knowledge establishes man's liberty rather than destroys it.

6. To defend the freedom of man's will, we should not deny God His perfection of knowledge. We may have to wait until the last day to better reconcile these two truths. Truly, "his ways [are] past finding out!" (Rom. 11:33). We should avoid fatalism on the one hand and atheism on the other.

How God Knows All Things

Once again, we find our limitations: only God knows all He knows, and only God knows how He knows all He knows. But we will make an attempt.

❖   God knows all things by His own essence. He does not have to look at things themselves, but rather to Himself, since He is the first cause of all things. He is not dependent on things for His knowledge. He knows all things in Himself.

❖   God knows all things by one act of intuition. He does not deduce one thing from another, as we do, and then draw His conclusions. He knows all things at once. There is no succession of thoughts with Him, no accumulation of knowledge. Time is all one to Him. He has the perfect vantage point from which to observe all.

❖ God knows all things independently. He needs no instructor to teach Him. "Who hath been his counselor?" (Rom. 11:34). As nothing He wills is the cause of His will, so nothing He knows is the cause of His knowledge. That which causes knowledge must exist before the knowledge. Since God's knowledge is eternal, nothing existed before Him to give Him knowledge of itself.

❖ God knows all things distinctly. "In him is no darkness at all" (John 1:5). He sees to the bottom of every issue. He knows the number of the hairs of our head. He is never confused. He is never distracted.

❖ God knows all things infallibly. There are no mistakes in His knowledge. He cannot be deceived. His knowledge is not a mere opinion, which is uncertain, but is the highest truth.

❖ God knows immutably. He cannot change as to His essence, and knowledge is one facet of His essence. Therefore, His knowledge cannot change. He cannot learn anything new, nor forget anything. His knowledge is eternally constant; it admits of no variation.

❖ God knows all things perpetually, that is, in one act. He does not know more at some times than others. There is never a lapse of knowledge with Him.

Proof That God Knows All Things

❖ He must know all we know and more. He cannot be exceeded by any creature or by all of them together. His perfection requires all knowledge. It is in terms of perfect knowledge that He is called "God only wise" (Rom. 16:27). No one can enjoy that which they do not understand; happiness is inconsistent with ignorance. As God has the highest enjoyment, He must know all things. Any degree of ignorance would render Him finite.

❖ All our knowledge is from Him. None of man's knowledge is innate. It is derived from the Creator. Psalm 94:10 asks, "He that teacheth man knowledge, shall not he know?" All our knowledge put together cannot equal His, which is boundless.

❖ The accusations of conscience prove that God knows all our actions. Even when no one on earth knows of our sins, our conscience condemns us. But why should we fear unless we know that there is a God who is keeping record? "For if our heart condemn us, God is greater than our heart, and knoweth all things" (1 John 3:20).

❖ God is the first cause of all things. Being a voluntary agent, He must be an intelligent agent. The faculty of will cannot exist without that of understanding also. His knowledge must extend as far as His operation. It is inconceivable that He should not thoroughly know what He has made.

❖ If God were not all knowing, He could no more govern than create the world. Knowledge is the basis of providence. Providence depends on the knowledge of God; the exercise of providence depends on the goodness of God. Without perfect knowledge, His justice could err. He who approvingly knows the way of the righteous also disapprovingly knows the way of the unrighteous (Ps. 1:6).

Now let us mark how we should apply this truth.

Information

The Lord Jesus Christ is not a mere creature. Two of His names, *Wonderful Counselor* and *Mighty God* (Isa. 9:6), indicate His perfect deity. He has a supreme knowledge of the Father, peculiar and essential to His nature, above that of which a creature is capable. "Neither knoweth any man the Father, save the Son" (Matt. 11:27). Moreover, the Holy Spirit knows all things; "He searcheth all things, yea, the deep things of God" (1 Cor. 2:10). And the Holy Spirit takes this knowledge from Christ: Jesus said, "All things that the Father hath are mine: therefore said I, that [the Holy Spirit] shall take of mine, and shall shew it unto you" (John 16:15). Therefore, Christ's knowledge must be complete. He also knows all creatures through and through. Colossians 2:3 declares, "In [Christ] are hid all the treasures of wisdom and knowledge." He knows the very hearts of men. "But Jesus did not commit himself unto them, because he knew all men, and needed not that any should testify of man: for he knew what was in man" (John 2:24–25). He knows all the inclinations and actions of men beforehand. "For Jesus knew from the beginning who they were that believed not, and who should betray him" (John 6:64). He knew Judas would betray and that Peter would deny.

God's providence is over all things because He knows all things. There is no heart but that He searches it; therefore, there is no heart but that He governs it. Nothing in the universe is so small that it escapes His providence, and nothing so sublime that it is above His understanding.

God's judgment is certain and right because of His knowledge. To give to every man according to his deeds, He must know all the deeds. He says, "I am he which searcheth the reins and hearts" (Rev. 2:23). He has set our secret sins in the light of His countenance (Ps. 90:8). Omniscience is a quality of which we see only a little now, but on the great day of judgment, it will be manifested fully.

This attribute gives ground for a final resurrection. Whether our body be eaten by worms or cannibals, God knows where to find its every part, and will raise it up at the last day. He knows every particle of matter in every place.

This attribute disproves any vain idea of justification by works. If we ourselves examine our works closely enough, we will find a flaw in every one. How much more does God see flaws in them! Well may we pray with David, "Enter not into judgment with thy servant: for in thy sight shall no man living be justified" (Ps. 143:2). Only a fool would dare to stand up and plead his own virtues before God.

This attribute furnishes us with much cause to worship God. We cannot but admire someone who knows more than we do, or who possesses insight concerning the future. How great God is in these respects! We should highly honor Him. Had He not fully known our need, His goodness could never have relieved us.

We should humble ourselves before God. Man is more apt to be proud of his knowledge than of anything else. Yet ours is nothing compared to God's. His knowledge should render Him honorable in our eyes and should render us vile. Recognizing that we possess more ignorance than knowledge, we ought to have low views of ourselves.

This attribute is much denied in this world. Adam thought he could escape God's knowledge by hiding. Cain pretended he knew not the whereabouts of Abel. All men wish God were not omniscient. We know God sees all things, but we live and walk as if He were blind. God says, "They consider not in their hearts that I remember all their wickedness: now their own doings have beset them about; they are before my face" (Hos. 7:2). Consider some ways this attribute is attacked.

When people pray to anyone other than God, as Romanists pray to saints, they attack God's unique omniscience. Prayer presupposes full knowledge on the part of the one to whom prayer is offered.

When people pry into what God has not revealed, they reveal their sinful ambition to be equal with God in knowledge. At the same time, they will overlook what has been revealed or what might be learned with a little effort. Swearing falsely or swearing by any creature shows contempt for God.

When we judge the hearts of men, we take to ourselves prerogatives that belong to God alone, as if we knew everything. "Therefore judge nothing before the time, until the Lord come, who both will bring to light the hidden things of darkness, and will make manifest the counsels of the hearts" (1 Cor. 4:5). We must judge actions, but we must leave the final assessment to God.

Some attack this attribute by abusing it. They say, "Why should we pray to God when He already knows everything?" They think prayer is for the purpose of administering knowledge to God. However, prayer is the expression of our desires, so that we might rightly honor God when He answers our requests and gives us what we need.

Every time a sin is committed, there is a disdain for God's omniscience. Or we may refrain from a sin because of the presence of a fellowman, perhaps a child. Thus, we show greater honor to a child's knowledge than to God's. Sins committed in secret are doubly evil, for they are against God's law as well as against His omniscience.

Making a partial confession of sin betrays contempt for God's knowledge, as if He knew nothing more than what we furnish Him with. If you would glorify this attribute, which shall one day break open your conscience, offer to God a full and sincere confession.

Merely external worship insults Omniscience. When there is a contradiction between our lips and our hearts, we flatter God as if He were a babe to be pacified with rattles and noises. But it is we and not He who are the deceived.

When we cherish evil thoughts, we reveal a lack of concern or respect for God's knowledge.

When we neglect prayer, we act as if God did not notice our sin of omission.

When we make hypocritical excuses to God to be exempted from obedience, as did Moses at the burning bush, we show a low view of Divine omniscience.

Comfort

God is fully aware of the enemies His people face. We can say, "Mine adversaries are all before thee" (Ps. 69:19). God saw the taskmasters in Egypt (Ex. 3:7). To the Assyrian king Sennacherib, God said, "But I know thy abode, and thy going out, and thy coming in, and thy rage against me" (Isa. 37:28). He knows our enemies better than we do.

God is worthy of our trust because He knows everything. His pity and power would be inoperative without His knowledge of our need. We can depend fully on Him because of the fullness of His knowledge.

God knows each of His people personally and intimately. We are not forgotten nor lost in the crowd. If He calls the stars by name (Ps. 147:4), how much more His own elect. Christ says, "I know my sheep" (John 10:27). "The Lord knoweth them that are His" (2 Tim. 2:19). God also sees the wolves that disguise themselves as sheep and mingle with the fold.

God's knowledge is a comfort to a sincere heart. What a comfort to know that God knows! Happy is the man who, like Job, can appeal with a clear conscience to the All-knowing. "Behold, my witness is in heaven, and my record is on high" (Job 16:19). Hezekiah could pray, "Remember now how I have walked before thee in truth and with a perfect heart, and have done that which is good in thy sight" (2 Kings 20:3).

We should be comforted by the fact that God knows our secret prayers and sighs and works, to which others are not privy. He knows our every good desire. "Lord, all my desire is before thee; and my groaning is not hid from thee" (Ps. 38:9). He is able to hear the cries of all His children on the earth at once.

God knows all our afflictions. To the Smyrna church He said, "I know thy works, and tribulation" (Rev. 2:9). He knows when the best time is to give afflictions for our good, and when to remove them. He saw Jonah in the belly of the whale and Daniel in the den of the lions. Under all the injustices of man, the saints may commit themselves to God with this assurance.

God knows all our infirmities. He knows the weakness of our nature, and pities us. "He knoweth our frame; he remembereth that we are dust" (Ps. 103:14). He remembers our mutable nature in our original creation. He knows our weakness in our sinful state. He knows our dependence on Him even in our regenerate state.

He knows our sins and reveals them to us so we might repent of them. "Search me, O God, and know my heart: try me, and know my thoughts" (Ps. 139:23). We may not only appeal to this attribute when others question our integrity, we may also appeal to it when we ourselves question our integrity. It comforts a young artist to have a skillful eye to critique his work. God's knowledge helps us in our self-examination for our good.

God knows all our sins, even those we do not see. His pardon in Christ is according to His knowledge, not ours. But if He were like us and knew only a part of our sins, we could never enjoy a full forgiveness. Also, God alone knows the fullness of Christ's merit. Thus, His omniscience does not stir up His justice against us. Rather, it stirs up His mercy. Herein is immense comfort!

To Sinners

God's knowledge speaks terrible things to the lost. He knows every deed, whisper, and thought. How much better would it be to have all your sins known by angels in heaven, men on earth, and devils in hell, rather than by God, the Lawgiver and Judge! There is no place to hide from Him. Achan could hide the gold from Joshua but not from God. "Thou hast set our iniquities before thee, our secret sins in the light of thy countenance" (Ps. 90:8). God is invisible to us, but we should not imagine that we are invisible to Him. The woman at the well of Samaria could bear witness to this. God's knowledge destroys the refuge of the hypocrite. "The LORD seeth not as man seeth; for man looketh on the outward appearance, but the LORD looketh on the heart" (1 Sam. 16:7). He can spy out Herod's murder veiled in a pretense of worship, Judas' treason in a kiss, and the Pharisees' fraud under a broad phylactery. Hypocrisy is a vain and futile exercise.

Furthermore, God has not forgotten one sin, no matter how long ago committed. The record stands in heaven except it be blotted out by the blood of Christ. Nor is God a mere spectator but a diligent observer. "The ways of man are before the eyes of the LORD, and he pondereth all his goings" (Prov. 5:21). He counted the times that Israel murmured against Him (Num. 14:22). He takes notice of the mercy against which men sin. The whole guilt is spread before Him. He will make use of His knowledge in judgment against the wicked. "Thou beholdest mischief and spite, to requite it with thy hand" (Ps. 10:14). Who can seriously consider all the sins of one day, of one year, of a whole lifetime, without inexpressible horror?

Exhortation

Let us have within our hearts a sense of God's all-seeing eye. All sin begins with failure in this. God said to Ezekiel, "Son of man, hast thou seen what the ancients of the house of Israel do in the dark, every man in the chambers of his imagery? for they say, The LORD seeth us not; the LORD hath forsaken the earth" (8:12). When we say to ourselves, "God does not know," we open the floodgates of sin. When a whole society thinks this way, that society cannot last long.

Remembering this attribute reaps many benefits:

❖ *It will keep us from many a sin by deadening us to temptation.* How can we yield to temptation when we know it will be booked in God's knowledge? Who would dare to utter a word of treason if he knew the king were listening?

❖ *It will make us watchful over our thoughts.* Not one of our millions of thoughts escapes God's view.

❖ *It will transform our service and worship.* We cannot fool God when we are sloppy about our duty. We should prepare our hearts to pray and hear by remembering beforehand the fact of His presence.

❖ *It will make us sincere and careful in our conduct.* David admonished Solomon, "Know thou the God of thy father, and serve him with a perfect heart and with a willing mind: for the LORD searcheth all hearts, and understandeth all the imaginations of the thoughts" (1 Chron. 28:9). Let us walk carefully before God, so that we might say with the psalmist, "I have kept thy precepts and thy testimonies: for all my ways are before thee" (119:168).

❖ *It will make us humble.* Consider all your provocations, injuries, blasphemies, doubts, lusts, omissions, and worms in your best fruit. Then consider God's patience and kindness, in spite of all the dross. Melt in humility before Him. If we know enough to render ourselves vile in our own eyes, how much more does God know to render us vile in His eyes!

❖ *It will make us rely on God in every circumstance.* He knows what is best for us. Therefore, let us confidently and joyfully commit ourselves to His keeping.

9

THE WISDOM OF GOD

Romans 16:27 says, "To God only wise, be glory through Jesus Christ for ever. Amen." Wisdom is here attributed to God alone. It is His unique property. No creature can lay claim to it. So wise is God that He is wisdom itself. Therefore, as the verse says, God is worthy of our worship.

Though most people confuse knowledge and wisdom, they are distinct, as we shall see.

What Wisdom Is

Wisdom consists in acting for a right end. God has determined that end and is presently using appropriate means to bring it to pass. "For of him, and through him, and to him, are all things: to whom be glory for ever. Amen" (Rom. 11:36).

Perfect wisdom necessitates perfect knowledge of all circumstances, so as never to be mistaken. Knowledge is the foundation of wisdom. Some men may have a measure of knowledge without wisdom. Wisdom takes knowledge and skillfully puts it to the best use according to a right judgment of things. Scripture itself makes some distinction between knowledge and wisdom in Romans 11:33, "O the depth of the riches both of the wisdom and knowledge of God!"

Some Propositions Concerning the Wisdom of God

First, we should distinguish between the *essential* wisdom of God and the *personal* wisdom of God. His essential wisdom is that quality which is His essence or nature. His personal wisdom is the person of Jesus Christ. "Christ the power of God, and the wisdom of God" (1 Cor. 1:24).

Second, wisdom is not a feature added to God's essence—it is His essence. Without it, He is not God. All God's perfections are one in Him. Though we consider one perfection at a time, as if distinct from others, we should understand that God is simple and not compound.

Third, God's wisdom is transcendent and infinite. "God only wise," says the Apostle. All other persons are at best philosophers. The title *philosopher* (or lover of wisdom) arose from a respect to God, who alone is worthy of the title *sophos* (or wise). Let us mark some ways in which God is wise:

❖ *God is wise necessarily.* Wisdom is inseparable from Him. It is the first vital operation of God.

❖ *He is wise originally.* All other wisdom derives from Him, but He derives it from no other.

❖ *He is wise perfectly.* By contrast, even the angels' wisdom is limited and, thus, imperfect.

❖ *He is wise universally.* He knows everything about everything and puts this knowledge to the best use.

❖ *He is wise perpetually*, unlike man who gains wisdom with age only to become decrepit and lose it again.

❖ *He is wise incomprehensibly.* His judgments are unsearchable, and His ways past finding out (Rom. 11:33). There is no limit as to how He might demonstrate His wisdom to us.

❖ *He is wise infallibly.* There is no error in Him. The wisest plot of an angel against Him is doomed to fail and will only fulfill God's purpose. "There is no wisdom nor understanding nor counsel against the LORD" (Prov. 21:30).

Proof That God Is Wise

"Wisdom and might are his," declares Daniel 2:20. There is no uncertainty or recklessness about God. If He needed to, He could give a satisfactory reason for His every decree. Let us consider some proofs of His wisdom.

1. *God could not be perfect without wisdom.* Wisdom is the most eminent and distinguished of His attributes. Without wisdom, all other virtues are rendered imperfect: patience becomes cowardice, power becomes oppression, justice becomes cruelty.

2. *God could not govern the world without wisdom.* It would be only chaos and confusion. God defended His sovereignty to Job by calling him to consider His great wisdom and power in the creating and governing of all things.

3. *The harmony by which all creation works for one end, even without their knowledge of it, demonstrates the wisdom of God.* We see this both through the microscope as well as the telescope.

4. *God is the source of all our wisdom.* Our excellence of wisdom is but an image of an infinitely superior excellence of wisdom in God. "He giveth wisdom unto the wise, and knowledge to them that know understanding" (Dan. 2:21). Our little wisdom argues for greater wisdom in Him.

Where We See God's Wisdom

Where do we see God's wisdom? First, we see it in creation. "The LORD by wisdom hath founded the earth" (Prov. 3:19). Consider the variety in creation. "O LORD, how manifold are thy works! in wisdom hast thou made them all" (Ps. 104:24). We see an almost endless diversity of shapes, colors, smells, sounds, and configurations. What an artist God is! Consider the beauty of all creation. "He hath made every thing beautiful in his time" (Eccl. 3:11). God could have made everything plain and bland, but the beauty and order of creation display His wisdom. Consider how all things are useful and fit for the end to which they were made. Nothing is unprofitable; everything serves some purpose. The heavens, the earth, the seas, plants, animals—they all tell of His wisdom. Man himself is a great testimony as well. We are wonderfully made (Ps. 139:14), both body and soul. Finally, consider how all creation links together to one common end. God in wisdom has made everything interdependent. The rain cycle and the food chain are good examples. How often do the Psalms speak of God's glory and wisdom in creation! And how often ought we to admire God and be humbled before Him who by wisdom has made these things!

Second, we see God's wisdom in His government of His creation. If someone picks up a musical instrument and plays a beautiful melody, it reflects the ability of the musician. Likewise, as we look at what God does with creation, we see His great wisdom. Though we could mention a host of other examples, we will confine ourselves to God's crowning work of creation—man.

God wisely governs man as a rational creature. He gave His law, which is "holy and just and good" (Rom. 7:12), perfectly suited to the special rational and moral nature of man. Adam was capable of obeying this law. It was a law well suited to the happiness and benefit of man. The whole law could be summarized with one word: love. Man's conscience approves of this law. God in wisdom gave incentives for its keeping. Had man obeyed this law, how happy would the world have been! Furthermore, God showed His wisdom by giving us His written revelation to keep us from error. Everywhere we look, we see God's wisdom in His government of man—even in the variety of personalities, skills, and economic conditions of mankind.

God wisely governs man as a sinful creature. Even though sin is in itself evil and tends to destroy the glory of God, God orders it and overrules it so that some greater good may come. He sets a bound upon sin lest earth become a hell. "Surely the wrath of man shall praise thee: the remainder of wrath shalt thou restrain" (Ps. 76:10). He brings glory to Himself from sin. He permitted Adam's fall so He might show more fully His own nature in redemption. How else could we have known God's infinite goodness, mercy, power, justice, and wisdom, without the stage of sin upon which they act? God also makes use of sinful instruments. He turns the devil's own scheme against him. He defeats him with his own weapons. What wisdom is needed to make things serve a purpose contrary to their nature! Using demons to carry out His ultimate purpose is more amazing than employing elect angels. He used the ambition and covetousness of the Assyrians to carry out justice against Judah. "O Assyrian, the rod of mine anger, and the staff in their hand is mine indignation. I will send him against an hypocritical nation, and against the people of my wrath will I give him a charge, to take the spoil, and to take the prey, and to tread them down like the mire of the streets. Howbeit he meaneth not so, neither doth his heart think so; but it is in his heart to destroy and cut off nations not a few" (Isa. 10:5–7). Again, we see God's wisdom in bringing good to creatures from sin. He willed to permit sin for wise purposes, which man or angel could never have imagined, nor which sin on its own could ever have attained. The fall of man was God's occasion to raise him higher than his created state. The violating of the old covenant was the occasion for a better one. The sin of the first Adam was the occasion for the righteousness of the second Adam. The Jews' unbelief was the occasion of the Gentiles' believing. Indwelling sin in a believer is the occasion to learn humility, dependence, a deeper appreciation for the blood and righteousness of Christ, and a greater zeal to strive for God's glory. Though sin naturally makes us fit for hell, God so overrules it as to make us fit for heaven. We come to hate sin all the more, to be more watchful lest we sin even more, to mortify sin increasingly, to strive for sanctification, to grow in grace. Thus, although God is not the author of sin, He is the administrator of it, and by His wisdom accomplishes marvelous purposes.

God wisely governs man as a redeemed creature. He takes the rubbish of the world and transforms it into a vessel of honor. He generally passes by the noble and mighty and saves those who seem most unfit. His timing shows wisdom: He waits until the best season to call by His grace. He then works through the Word in the rational faculties of man's soul, effectually yet agreeably, opening man's will without injuring the nature of the will. Furthermore, God shows His wisdom in disciplining His children and in punishing His enemies. The church is never more like heaven than when it is persecuted by hell. God outwits Satan by purifying His people through that which was intended to pollute us. The afflictions of the saints are for the furtherance of the gospel (Phil. 1:12). Over and over, "the wicked is snared in the work of his own hands" (Ps. 9:16). The very gods of Egypt become a plague. Giant Goliath is leveled with a small stone. The deliverance of the Jewish captives hinges on one sleepless night for King Ahasuerus. Saul the Pharisee is perfectly suited to expose Judaism after his conversion. What a wise architect God is!

Third, we see God's wisdom in redemption. Here is the height of wisdom, beyond all that which is demonstrated in creation and providence. Colossians 2:3 says that "in Christ are hid all the treasures of wisdom and knowledge." This wisdom is hidden from the eyes of natural man. It is called "the hidden wisdom" (1 Cor. 2:7). Even the angels did not perceive it beforehand: "To the intent that now unto the principalities and powers in heavenly places might be known by the church the manifold wisdom of God" (Eph. 3:10). This wisdom is also *manifold* or multifaceted; various counsels meet in the wonder of redemption. Let us consider the display of God's wisdom in redemption:

1. God in wisdom *reconciles justice and mercy*. Justice presents its case: "The sinner is miserable because of his own willful rebellion. He was created perfect. He has no excuse. He cannot plead ignorance. If he is not punished, the holy law will be overthrown in

disgrace and the devil's lie will be approved. The crime cannot be passed over. After all, what is to keep him from sinning again?" But mercy pleads its case: "Will all creation be in vain—ending in judgment and destruction? Was not man tempted, after all? Was he not made mutable? Will Satan be victorious with every one of Adam's race? Will I never appear on the stage to display my beauty?" Forthwith, truth comes to the aid of justice, and grace comes to the aid of mercy. But God in wisdom devises a scheme to satisfy both parties: Christ the Son of God atones for man. Therefore, neither side has ground for complaint. "Mercy and truth are met together; righteousness and peace have kissed each other" (Ps. 85:10). Instead of an unrighteous mercy or a merciless justice, there is a righteous mercy and a merciful justice.

2. God in wisdom *makes the Son to be the Redeemer*. The great truth of the Trinity comes into view here. It was not appropriate that the Father, the Judge Himself, should take the office of Mediator or be sent by the Son and punished by the Son. Nor was it appropriate that the Holy Spirit be the Mediator, seeing He eternally proceeds from the Father and the Son and should not precede the Son in the work of redemption. Rather, the Spirit applies the Son's work in the hearts of men. It is the Son who is best suited for the office of Mediator. By Him all things were created, so by Him all things are made new. He is the Word, so He may speak on our behalf. He is the only begotten and beloved, so He may intercede for us. He is the Son, so He may introduce us into a state of adoption. Who could better mediate than God the Son?

3. God in wisdom *united two natures*, divine and human, in one person to accomplish redemption. How amazing that such unlike things should be joined! Only incomprehensible wisdom could ever unite the finite with the infinite, power with weakness, immortality with mortality, immutability with mutability. He who is eternally spirit partakes of flesh and blood. The lawgiver is made under the law. He who was in the bosom of the Father is joined with the

womb of His mother. Yet each nature remains distinct so that there is no mixture. Nor is the divine nature altered in any way by the adding of the human nature. This union was full, personal, and perpetual. "For in him dwelleth all the fulness of the Godhead bodily" (Col. 2:9). Thus, Christ is perfectly and uniquely fitted to be a Mediator between God and men because He personally knows things pertaining to God as well as the infirmities of man (Heb. 5:1; 4:15). Had He not been man, He could not have taken our place in suffering. Had He not been God, His sufferings would have had no merit to apply to us. Had He been only man, He could not have assured us an approach to God. Had He been only God, His justice would not have allowed us an approach to Him. He has a nature for our comfort as well as a nature for our confidence. What glorious wisdom we see in the incarnation!

4. God in wisdom *arranged the vindication of His law*, both as to its precept and as to its penalty. The first Adam had this precept: to freely eat of every tree except one. He also had this penalty: "In the day that thou eatest thereof thou shalt surely die" (Gen. 2:17). Since Adam sinned, the penalty was enforced. But what of the precept? Would God's command never be obeyed? Here again we see God's wisdom, in that He made a way to satisfy both the precept and the penalty. Christ fulfills the precept of the law by His active obedience and suffers the penalty of the law by His passive obedience. God's wonders of wisdom are beyond our imagination!

5. God in wisdom *manifests contrary affections at the same time in one act*. Redemption reveals His greatest hatred against sin and His greatest love to the sinner. No act of God so demonstrates His holy hatred like His punishing of His own Son when He took the guilt of sinners to the cross. No act of God so demonstrates His love like His imputing to those sinners the very righteousness of Christ and bringing them to heaven as sons and daughters.

6. God in wisdom *defeats the devil by using the very means introduced by the devil*. Through man, Satan destroyed creation. But through man, namely the God-man, Satan and his plans were destroyed. "For since by man came death, by man came also the resurrection of the dead" (1 Cor. 15:21). Though Satan was the instrument of death on the earth, the death of Christ dealt the mortal blow to Satan. Through death, our Lord destroyed "him that had the power of death" (Heb. 2:14). Satan turned original glory into shame, but God in wisdom turned shame into a glory greater than the original.

7. God in wisdom *secures both our comfort as well as our obedience*. By the same blood, God is satisfied, and the sinner is sanctified. Nothing so serves to deliver us from despair and wean us from sin like a crucified Christ. Nothing motivates us to obedience like the knowledge of being already reconciled to God. The grace of God teaches us to deny ungodliness and worldly lusts (Titus 2:11–12). Christ Himself is made our supreme example in holiness. A pattern to be imitated is greater than a law to be ruled by.

8. God in wisdom *has made faith to be the condition necessary to the receiving and enjoying of the benefits of redemption*. Faith does not require a sinless believer; otherwise, we would have no hope as sinners. Works could never have been the condition of the covenant, seeing man was in a fallen state and incapable of good works. Nor is faith a work of merit; rather, it is consistent with grace. It humbles man and gives all glory to God. Since unbelief was the condition of our fall, it is only reasonable that belief be the condition of our restoration. Also, faith and repentance answer to the deepest conscience of man. Since sin operates deeply in us, so does the grace of faith. Furthermore, we were united to the first Adam by natural generation, but our union with Christ must be by a spiritual connection. Faith is suited to such a connection since it involves the whole soul of man: understanding, emotion, and will.

9. God in wisdom *determined how to make known the truth of redemption*. Man's weakness could not stand a sudden revelation of
it, so God opened it to man gradually. He began in Genesis 3:15
to Adam. Then He revealed more through Abraham, and more
through Moses, yet even more through David, and more through
the prophets. Finally, it was unveiled by Christ and His apostles. The
means God used to reveal His truth render it easy to believe. Many
detailed prophecies were given concerning Christ. By the transla-
tion of the Old Testament in Greek, the world was able to read
the truth before the birth of Christ. The historical facts of the life
and death and resurrection of Christ were indisputable to the first-
century world. Likewise, they are indisputable to this very day. God
even preserved in man's thought, whether Jewish or pagan, certain
principles, such as the necessity of sacrifice and the possibility of an
incarnation. But it was the crucifixion that became the stumbling
block to both Jews and Gentiles. God showed His wisdom in the
timing and method of the first great ingathering of souls, at Pen-
tecost, where devout people were gathered from all over the world
who witnessed the gift of tongues. The gospel was given not to philosophers but to fishermen that the success of the truth might not
be credited to man's ingenuity and contrivance but to God's power
alone. When we see such feeble instruments proclaiming a doctrine
repugnant to sinful flesh, a crucified Savior who demands our submission and self-denial, who calls us to suffer reproach and affliction, and when we see this message meet with any success, we can
only marvel in God's wisdom. He had prepared for the spreading of
the gospel by the Jewish dispersion. He facilitated the evangelizing
of the world through the persecution in Jerusalem (Acts 8:4). The
flames of martyrs only brighten the dark corners. The imprisonment
of the ark becomes the downfall of Dagon. God wisely carries on
His work in this way so that less of humanity and more of divinity
might appear.

Now let us consider what we should learn from this marvelous
attribute.

Information

We learn something of the deity of Christ. Wisdom is one of His titles. "Christ the power of God, and the wisdom of God" (1 Cor. 1:24). He is wisdom personified in Proverbs 8:12–36. He created all and is judge of all, and so He must be all-wise.

We learn that God is rightly fitted to govern the world. In public affairs, we look for the wisest man to be governor or magistrate. How much more fit is God because of His wisdom? In wisdom He made all the earth (Ps. 104:24). He who made all things is most suited to continue to guide and govern all things.

We learn the ground of God's patience: He is patient because He is wise. Men who are weak are impatient; they sense that they are outmatched. But a wise man bears patiently, knowing that he will attain his end. God makes all things to work together for good. He is in no hurry. He bore with the sins of Old Testament saints knowing He would send His Son to atone for them.

We learn the immutability of God's decrees. His wisdom is eternal; therefore, He determined the very best thing to do. Man sometimes fails in his promises due to ignorance and folly. But God never fails nor alters any of His plan since there is no folly in Him, only wisdom.

We learn that God is worthy of our trust. No unforeseen problems can arise with Him. He cannot overextend Himself in His promises, as some well-meaning men do.

We learn the importance of the public judgment at the end of the world. Many riches of wisdom and other attributes will be shown in splendor on that day and not before. God will be honored as all beings behold the wisdom of His dealings reviewed on that day.

We learn good reasons for reverencing and worshiping God. We admire a wise man who makes a complicated machine. We ought to stand in awe of God who in wisdom made the universe.

But even more, we ought to bow in wonder and praise to Him for the greater work of redemption.

We learn our need of seeking Him for guidance. Since He is all-wise, He is our best counselor. He is "great in counsel, and mighty in work" (Jer. 32:19). We often seek advice from wise men, but most of all, we need God's assistance and wisdom.

Conviction

Man in sin degrades God's wisdom. Satan wants to be God's equal in power, but man wants to be God's equal in wisdom. All sin strikes against this attribute in one of two ways. First, by defacing the wise workmanship of God. All sin is destructive; it is an insult against the sovereign Creator. Second, sin always slights God's laws, calling into question the wisdom of His rule. We pay lip service to His wisdom, but every time we disobey, we are accusing Him of folly or incompetence in what He has instructed us to do. In effect we say, "I know better than God what is good for me." But to contradict the highest wisdom is to prove ourselves to be fools. Thus, one of the most common synonyms in Scripture for a sinner is *fool*, and for sin, *folly*. Consider some ways God's wisdom is defied:

❖ *By introducing innovations in worship*, like the strange fire of Nadab and Abihu.

❖ *By neglecting the means God has appointed and seeking some more pleasing way*, like Naaman, who thought he had better waters than the Jordan in which to wash. How many men fail to submit to Christ for righteousness or to look to God for direction!

❖ *By criticizing God's revelations and actions*, setting up our own reason in place of God's wisdom. The critic always speaks from a position of superiority. "The Bible is beneath my intelligence," he says. If we had to know all God's reasons for His actions, we would become His equals, either by ascending to His wisdom or reducing Him to ours.

❖ *By telling God what He should do.* We must be careful in our praying not to dictate to God as if we knew best and as if He should submit to our orders. Saul lost a kingdom because he thought he knew better than God what to do with the cattle of the Amalekites.

❖ *By murmuring and impatience.* "Why must I suffer like this?" people often ask. "Why must it last so long?" They might as well say, "God does not know what He is doing." Discontentment betrays a suspicious heart against God.

❖ *By entertaining a proud, lofty opinion of ourselves.* We then expect others to agree with us and hold us in high regard. We want them to esteem us higher than they esteem God. Thus, we invert God's order and charge Him with lack of wisdom. But the thought of God humbles every man in the dust.

❖ *By unbelief.* All distrust of God's Word is an impeachment of His wisdom.

Comfort

God conducts all the affairs of His children in infinite wisdom. His wisdom inflicts our troubles, and His wisdom removes them. Both distresses and deliverances are fruits of His wisdom for our good. Like a skilled physician, He suits the medicine to our disease, not to our desire. Our Lord was tempted and thus became familiar with the feeling of our infirmities (Heb. 4:15). Paul sought deliverance from his thorn, but through feeling the thorn, he was kept conscious of the power of Christ (2 Cor. 12:9).

When God denies our prayers or delays in answering them, He does so in wisdom. Perhaps He waits so we might more highly value the answer when it comes. His timing is best, and He will give the best covenant mercy to His people. Though enemies threaten, assail, and even injure us, God's wisdom prevails. "There is no wisdom nor understanding nor counsel against the Lord" (Prov. 21:30).

We do not question a sculptor's wisdom when he takes up the file instead of the polish. Likewise, fear not when God takes up His files and axes—He knows how to use them skillfully. He loves us too much to destroy us, and He can beautify us with the roughest of tools.

Exhortation

Let us meditate much on God's wisdom manifested in creation and providence. Everywhere we observe, we see amazing wisdom. Yet how many of these things we take for granted! Failing to glorify God as Creator was the first step in the downward spiral described in Romans 1. God created these things more for His glory than for our use. We ourselves were created to bring glory to Him, not merely to look at ourselves. If we fail to behold His glory through creation, we become no better than brute beasts. Meditating on creation increases our humility.

Psalm 8 declares, "When I consider thy heavens, the work of thy fingers, the moon and the stars, which thou hast ordained; What is man, that thou art mindful of him? and the son of man, that thou visitest him?" (vv. 3–4). We are so small and ignorant! We could never have designed such things, let alone had the power to form them. Also, we must see God's great goodness to us in making us in His likeness, above the rest of creation. As we meditate on creation, we see illustrations of the greater work of redemption. For example, Christ is called a lamb and a lion. If we can see the glory of God in creation, we begin to enjoy heaven on earth, for in our glorified state, we shall enjoy a new heaven and earth unspoiled by sin and its effects. Adam had only a short time to see creation in its perfection, but we will have all eternity to see even better things.

Let us study and admire the wisdom of God in redemption. This is worthy of our utmost effort. We must not neglect necessary earthly duties, nor must we neglect to grow in the knowledge of God. Indeed, such study will prompt us to our duties. Our eternal occupation will be to admire and praise and delight in God. His wisdom in redemption is an ocean waiting for us to take one cupful at a time and marvel in it. How inquisitive are the elect angels! And will we be careless to discover the riches of God's grace? Let us take pains to be students of God. "Learn of Me," our Savior said. What hope would we have had without Him?

Let us not dare to be proud of or trust in our own wisdom. By pretending to be wiser than God, the world was ruined. This should humble us. What has six thousand years of human history proven, except that man is simply blind! If we do not trust ourselves, we will more likely look to another—God—for direction. Let us acknowledge our folly. "Let no man deceive himself. If any man among you seemeth to be wise in this world, let him become a fool, that he may be wise" (1 Cor. 3:18).

Let us seek wisdom from God. "If any of you lack wisdom, let him ask of God . . . and it shall be given him" (James 1:5). God has wisdom for our salvation as well as for our daily life. But those who go with Saul to the witch of Endor will get counsel from hell.

Let us submit to God's wisdom in all cases. We must empty ourselves and submit to His written revelation concerning Himself and all things. We must be content with what He has not revealed; this also is according to His wisdom. We must submit to His methods of accomplishing His will. A half-blind man is a poor judge of God's ways. We must submit to all the crosses He gives us to bear. Pleasant things are often not good for us. The thing we long for may destroy us. Bodily health might prove to be a disease to our souls. Earthly riches might leave us heavenly paupers. Rachel said she would die if she had no children, but she died giving birth (Gen. 30:1; 35:18). Better to leave it to God to choose what is best for us.

Let us not murmur against God in any of His dealings. We can only guess at what His specific designs may be in any occurrence. When He reveals something, He also hides something. He said to Peter, "What I do thou knowest not now; but thou shalt know hereafter" (John 13:7). Like Peter, we must be content to wait on Him. Rather than complain, we should acquiesce and adore. In the end, when God's whole scheme is unraveled to our minds, we will see that He has done all things well. In the meantime, let us anticipate that day and praise Him as the only wise God.

10

THE POWER OF GOD

Infinite and incomprehensible power pertains to God's nature, and is expressed, in part, in His works. Job by inspiration declared, "Lo, these are parts of his ways: but how little a portion is heard of him? but the thunder of his power who can understand?" (26:14). We ought not to think God's power is limited to the actions He performs. His actions show only a part of His essential power. David wrote, "God hath spoken once; twice have I heard this; that power belongeth unto God" (Ps. 62:11). Seventy times in Scripture God is called *Almighty*.

God and power are so inseparable that they are reciprocal terms. In Mark 14:62, our Lord said He would "sit on the right hand of power." In chapter 16:19, we read He "sat on the right hand of God."

What God's Power Is

Strength to act is one simple definition of God's power. But we should also mention the right or authority to exercise that strength, for one may act in power without proper authority, or one may have proper authority but be hindered from acting. But God has both authority and ability to act.

God possesses both absolute and ordinate power. His absolute power speaks of all He might do but has not determined to do. His ordinate power speaks of all He has decreed to do. In His absolute power, He could have kept Adam from sin. He could have raised up children to Abraham from mere stones. He could have sent twelve legions of angels to rescue Christ from the cross. But His ordinate power, according to His will, was to do none of these things. He had better plans. God is able to accomplish whatever He pleases and designs without any difficulty or resistance. His power is as great as His will. And since power is the principle of action, it is therefore greater than any action itself. Unlike us, God depends on nothing to show His power. He needs no object at hand in the first place or any means available by which to work.

From our perspective, this power is distinct from God's wisdom and will. His will orders, His wisdom guides, and His power accomplishes. As Ephesians 1:11 puts it, He works all things according to the counsel of His own will. Scripture tells us He has done whatever He pleased (Ps. 115:3), but it never tells us He has done whatever He could.

This attribute gives activity to all the other perfections of God's nature. Without power, His mercy would be a feeble pity, His promise an empty sound, His justice a mere scarecrow. In some respects, God's power is of a larger extent than other attributes. Mercy supposes a miserable object; justice supposes a criminal. But power actually constitutes an object. It creates and preserves. When mercy or justice cease, power continues to preserve the person either in hell or heaven.

God's power is essential to His being. The power of an earthly king is in his people, practically speaking. But God's power is in Himself. He needs no means by which to act. Man, on the other hand, constantly depends on the use of means. What little measure of power we have is derived from God. He alone is essentially almighty.

Since His essence is infinite, it follows that His power is infinite. We cannot tally the sum of our thoughts, yet He "is able to do exceeding abundantly above all that we ask or think" (Eph. 3:20).

He surpasses our arithmetic. There is nothing too hard for Him (Jer. 32:17). He works according to His will; His will is not limited by His power. He does not do the thousandth part of what He is able to do. But all He does He does perfectly according to what He has determined. That is not to say His will limits His power but that His will guides the demonstration of His power. He could have made a spider as strong as a lion, but He determined otherwise. All His designs and use of His power are in perfect wisdom. Also, His power never diminishes. "Hast thou not known? hast thou not heard, that the everlasting God, the Lord, the Creator of the ends of the earth, fainteth not, neither is weary?" (Isa. 40:28). Thus, His power is infinite and is called "His eternal power" (Rom. 1:20).

The fact that there are some things God cannot do in no way diminishes His power; rather, it strengthens it. Some things are impossible in their own nature. For example, to be and not to be at the same time is an impossibility. That which is done cannot be undone. Some things are impossible to the nature of God. For one, He cannot cease to be what He is; He cannot contradict His own essence. He cannot die. Some things are impossible to the glorious perfections of God. For instance, He cannot sin. He cannot lie (Titus 1:2; Heb. 6:18). He cannot deny Himself (2 Tim. 2:13). Being weak in any of these areas would not be perfection but a lack thereof. Is a sweet fountain considered weak because it cannot send forth bitter water? Last of all, some things are impossible because God has ordained it so. For example, it was impossible that the world be destroyed immediately upon Adam's sin for God's decree before the foundation of the world was to restore a great multitude in Christ.

Proofs of God's Omnipotence

Of course, Scripture often asserts this truth. God answered Sarah's doubt with this question: "Is anything too hard for the Lord?" (Gen. 18:14). He answered Moses, who questioned how God would provide food for hungry Israel, with this question: "Is the LORD's hand waxed short?" (Num. 11:23). But let us consider some other arguments.

The power that creatures possess points to their Creator's power, which must be even greater. The source or cause must be greater than the effect. The original power must be all-powerful to effect all other things. All lesser powers are derived from the original.

Without infinite power, God would not be perfect. Any weakness would be a deficiency, a lack, which would make Him finite and not perfect. Pure power cannot be mixed with weakness. If God were not perfect in power, we could imagine some being more powerful and therefore more perfect than He. Such a suggestion is blasphemous.

The simplicity of God proves His power. A composite being may lose a faculty and diminish in power. For example, a man may lose an arm and with it lose some strength. But since God is a simple spirit, His power cannot be diminished.

The miracles God has wrought prove His power. All His works in nature manifest His power, but when some normal working of nature is reversed, men are struck with greater admiration than usual. For example, when the fire did not consume the three Hebrews inside the furnace but consumed the king's servants on the outside, Nebuchadnezzar was astonished and declared that there is no other God like Jehovah (Dan. 3:29). As Psalm 136:4 states, He "alone doeth great wonders." Yet, the greatest miracle demonstrates only a small part of His might.

Where God's Power Appears

1. *His power appears in creation.* The heaven is called "the firmament of his power" (Ps. 150:1). The first sentence of the Bible boldly expresses infinite power: "In the beginning God created the heaven and the earth."

This attribute is the first concept in the mind of creatures concerning their Creator, according to Romans 1:20, "For the invisible things of him from the creation of the world are clearly seen, being understood by the things that are made, even his eternal power and Godhead." In Scripture, the true God is often distinguished from false gods by the evidence of creation. They are called "the gods that have not made the heavens and the earth" (Jer. 10:11). But "our Lord is above all gods. Whatsoever the Lord pleased, that did he in heaven, and in earth, in the seas, and all deep places" (Ps. 135:5–6).

God showed His power by creating all things out of nothing. The only matter that has ever existed is that which He made. The distance between nothing and something, between not being and being, is immeasurable, spanned only by the almighty God. No greater power is conceivable to our minds. The best man can do is to rearrange matter; he never creates it. Consider also the extensive variety of creatures God made. First, He made matter, and then He formed it into an almost endless variety of distinct shapes and structures. A casual observer would not imagine it all came from one source. But God did all this with ease, without any instruments. He says, "I am the Lord that maketh all things; that stretcheth forth the heavens alone; that spreadeth abroad the earth by myself" (Isa. 44:24). Simply by an act of His will, He spoke the word, and it was so. "He spake, and it was done; he commanded, and it stood fast" (Ps. 33:9). He made the universe as easily as we form a thought. He could have made any number of worlds, had He desired. Moreover, He made all things instantaneously. No sooner had He spoken than it came to pass perfectly.

2. *God's power appears in His governing of the world.* This work may be divided into natural, moral, and gracious government.

In natural government, God first preserves. "O Lord, thou preservest man and beast" (Ps. 36:6). He says to the water of the seas, "Hitherto shalt thou come, but no further: and here shall thy proud waves be stayed" (Job 38:11). Nothing has power to preserve itself. Rather, the same power that created a thing must preserve it. If God ceased to preserve all things, they would return to nothing. Second, He propagates the creation. He causes the seed to grow and multiply. In reference to the propagation of man, the psalmist exclaims, "I will praise thee; for I am fearfully and wonderfully made: marvellous are thy works" (139:14). Scripture often speaks of God's opening and closing the womb. Third, He governs the motions of all creatures. "In Him . . . we move" (Acts 17:28). All motion, from the solar system to the circulatory system of man, is by His power. If He pleases, He can make the sun stand still or cause a man's heart to suddenly stop beating. Truly the power to preserve motion is just as great as the power to interrupt it.

In moral government, God restrains the malicious nature of the devil. If the devil were not restrained, earth would be turned into hell. He who first tempted Eve would assault all men as he did Job. He desired to sift Peter (Luke 22:31). But God governs all the actions of Satan. As Job said concerning God, "The deceived and the deceiver are his" (12:16). God also restrains the natural corruption of mankind. Every member of Adam's race is equally corrupt. We all branch from the same root. We are no better than Adam. It is dreadful to imagine what evils men would commit were God not hindering them. Romans 1 is a portrait of every one of us in our natural state. But God restrains us with His great power. Furthermore, He orders and guides the evil in the world to the accomplishing of His own ends. He allowed wicked men to crucify Christ. Yet, to preserve the early church from the same wicked men, God sent fear upon every soul (Acts 2:43). Thus, those who were bold to nail the Son of God to the cross were frightened at the appearance of twelve unarmed men. This is but one example of how God guides the evil He permits.

In gracious government, God shows His power by preserving His elect. In both Old Testament and New, many enemies have arisen against the people of God. How many laws and edicts arose, how many armies, how many dangers, how many betrayers from within the ranks, how many subtle maneuvers toward compromise! Yet God preserves. Satan thought he raised up Pharaoh to destroy the worshipers of God, but the truth was, God raised up Pharaoh to be an object lesson of His great power in the plagues He sent. He made His glorious name to be declared throughout all the earth in the reports of the Red Sea victory that circulated around the world (Rom. 9:17). In the end, there were more worshipers! In church history, God has wrought many deliverances for His people that are nothing short of miraculous. We continue to this day by His preserving power.

Consider the judicial proceedings of God as evidence of His governing. He judged Sodom by a shower of fire from heaven. He sets up monarchs by His power and by the same power brings them down. Mighty empires have disappeared due to surprising means, such as the Roman Empire trodden down by barbarians. All of nature is at His command. The sea that devoured not one Israelite did not spare one Egyptian. God delights to use small means to bring His governing purposes to pass, such as a squadron of lice to humble Pharaoh or a squadron of three hundred to defeat the Midianite hosts. Nothing is so small that God cannot do great things with it.

3. *God's power appears in redemption.* Surely His power is manifested in its highest heights here. Christ is called "the power of God" as well as "the wisdom of God" (1 Cor. 1:24). How much easier it would have been for God to create a new world than restore a broken one!

First, let us consider the person who accomplishes the redemption. It is none other than the God-man, the Lord Jesus Christ. As the eternal Son of God, He took flesh—but not sinful flesh. Supernaturally conceived by the Holy Spirit in the virgin's womb, this seed of the woman (Gen. 3:15) was perfectly and uniquely fitted to the office of mediator between God and men. In the previous chapter we spoke of the infinite wisdom displayed in the designing of the two natures united in one person. Now we speak of the actual accomplishing of that design as a display of infinite power. It involved the bringing together of natures very opposite and distant from each other. Yet the two natures were neither mixed nor changed. Our finite understanding cannot fully comprehend this union, but we can understand that divine power brought it to pass.

Moreover, we see a marvelous display of power in the life and ministry and death and resurrection of Christ. His many miracles speak for themselves. But perhaps the greatest wonder was His patience, by which He daily endured all the reproaches of men and especially their crimes against Him in conspiring His death. Again, in infinite power, God raised Him from the dead. Words seem inadequate for the Apostle as he expresses this lofty truth: "exceeding greatness of his power . . . mighty power, which he wrought in Christ, when he raised him from the dead" (Eph. 1:19–20).

Second, let us consider the publishing of the truth of redemption. When we look at the nature of the gospel message and the people who spread that message and the means they employed, we cannot help but see the exercise of divine power. The message flies in the face of man's natural wisdom. The philosophers at Athens considered a crucified and resurrected God an unreasonable teaching. They mocked the message and called the messenger a "babbler" (Acts 17:18). The Jews saw the message as contrary to their customs and a threat to their stability. They were just as devoted to their traditions as were the Gentiles to their superstitions. The gospel of Christ ultimately goes against the grain of every man, regardless of outward distinctions. What power is required to pry a man away from his sinful prejudices! He loathes nothing more than self-denial and utter humiliation in every area of his life. Hearing this message from common, uneducated spokesmen formerly employed in boats and nets made the truth even more incredible. And these lowly apostles dared accuse the dignified princes of this world of the murder of Jesus Christ! They did not use an army or the laws of the land to give success to their cause. They simply spoke the truth of God, without polished oratory, depending on a higher power for success. Never did a religion encounter such fierce opposition as did Christianity under the Romans. Yet, despite all this, the gospel turned the world upside down. In less than twenty years, every province of the empire had heard the message of the cross. Persecution only served to swell the number of believers. Even some of Nero's servants were converted (Phil. 4:22). To what can we credit the success of the gospel but to the power of its Author?

Third, let us consider the application of redemption. The power of God is most evident in this mighty work of conversion, which is compared to a creation, a birth, and a resurrection. Conversion is a radical transformation in which the heart of a man is turned against all its natural inclinations. The gospel, which is "the power of God unto salvation" (Rom. 1:16), finds a natural enemy in man's mind, heart, and will. It would be easier to turn a fly into an eagle than to turn a sinner into a saint. The claims of God go against all our deep-rooted, dominating habits. "Can the Ethiopian change his skin, or the leopard his spots? then may ye also do good, that are accustomed to do evil" (Jer. 13:23). But God works mightily to draw sinners to Himself (John 6:44). He dispossesses man of his self-esteem, hurls down his pride, subdues his passions, implants the fear of God where there was only contempt, makes him eager to serve his new Master, and grants desires for God's honor. No power less than divine can separate our heart from the world. How many bolted doors must Omnipotence break through to rescue us from ourselves! The power is so efficacious that nothing can stop it, yet it is so sweet that none did ever complain of it. "It is God which worketh in you both to will and to do of his good pleasure" (Phil. 2:13). He draws with cords of love (Jer. 31:3). He twists together victory and pleasure so that we delight to be conquered. Well did Peter write, "His divine power hath given unto us all things that pertain unto life and godliness" (2 Peter 1:3).

Not only is God's power demonstrated in the sinner but also in the pardon He grants. He exercises a power over Himself to bear with many injuries and to answer His own justice in the person of His Son.

Fourth, God's power is displayed in preserving His redeemed ones. It is one thing to subdue but another to maintain the subjugation. The power to keep under the yoke is no less than the power to impose the yoke in the first place. God magnifies His power by causing believers to persevere in the world, a weak and half-rigged vessel amid rocks and tempests, more than if He had immediately transported us to heaven.

Now let us apply this teaching.

Information and Instruction

Because Jesus Christ is all-powerful, and only God is all-powerful, Jesus must be God. "What things soever [the Father] doeth, these also doeth the Son likewise" (John 5:19)—not as two co-workers but rather as one essence, working one undivided operation. Repeatedly in Scripture the work of creation is credited to Christ the Son. "By whom also [God] made the worlds" (Heb. 1:2). "Thou, Lord, in the beginning hast laid the foundation of the earth; and the heavens are the works of thine hands" (Heb. 1:10). "By him were all things created, that are in heaven, and that are in earth, visible and invisible, whether they be thrones, or dominions, or principalities, or powers: all things were created by him, and for him" (Col. 1:16). "All things were made by him; and without him was not any thing made that was made" (John 1:3). He did not merely make some things, but *all things*. Therefore, He Himself was not created. Nor was the Son a mere instrument in creating but was the principal cause. He is further credited with preserving all things. "By Him all things consist" (Col. 1:17). The power to resurrect from the grave is credited to Him. "The Lord Jesus Christ . . . shall change our vile body, that it may be fashioned like unto his glorious body, according to the work-ing whereby he is able even to subdue all things unto himself" (Phil. 3:20–21). Let no one doubt His ability to save who has the power of creation, preservation, and resurrection in His hands.

Likewise, the Holy Spirit is God. He was active in creation: "And the Spirit of God moved upon the face of the waters" (Gen. 1:2). He is active in conversion: "For our gospel came not unto you in word only, but also in power, and in the Holy Ghost" (1 Thess. 1:5). He is active in resurrection: "But if the Spirit of him that raised up Jesus from the dead dwell in you, he that raised up Christ from the dead shall also quicken your mortal bodies by his Spirit that dwelleth in you" (Rom. 8:11).

We learn the blessedness of God. Since He is almighty, He can lack nothing. For any lack indicates weakness.

Here is ground for God's immutability. Nothing can force Him to change, for there is no power greater than His. The second psalm speaks of His laughing at any who challenge Him.

Here is ground for God's governing of the world. His knowl-edge and wisdom and power meet in the work of providence. Those who deny it would deny Him His head and heart and hands.

Here is ground for the worship of God. We admire strength, whether we see it in a human body or in an army of men. How much more shall we admire and adore the omnipotent God! All worship stands on two pillars: goodness and power in God. If either of these were defective, religion would vanish. On this ground we pray: "For thine is the kingdom and the power and the glory forever." When we forget this attribute, we become careless in worship.

Here is ground for believing in the resurrection. "With God nothing shall be impossible" (Luke 1:37). If He created us out of nothing, He could certainly gather our atoms from here and there at the last day.

It is strange that this attribute should be abused and held in contempt, as it is by sinful men. They deny that He created or that He is able to do all things. All sin, especially obstinate security in sin, is an attack against this attribute. Man imagines himself a match for God. "Do we provoke the Lord to jealousy? Are we stronger than He?" (1 Cor. 10:22). Every form of unbelief is but to assume that God can do no more than we. The nation that crossed the Red Sea soon asked, "Can God furnish a table in the wilderness?" (Ps. 78:19). How often practical atheism asserts itself! We doubt God's power when we fear man. "Who art thou, that thou shouldest be afraid of a man that shall die, and of the son of man which shall be made as grass; and forgettest the LORD thy maker, that hath stretched forth the heavens, and laid the foundations of the earth?" (Isa. 51:12–13). Trusting self rather than God betrays a scorning of God's power. Ascribing good to the means He provides rather than to Himself amounts to an insult against His power.

But we should not abuse the doctrine by using it to justify contradictions. For example, some argue for the false doctrine of transubstantiation by saying, "God is able to change the bread and wine into the literal body and blood of the Lord." We might as well believe Aesop's fables! God's power does not contradict His word. Nor should we presume on God's power by neglecting to use the means He provides. God's power should never be an excuse for our idleness or disobedience. On the other hand, rushing into danger is more an abuse of God's power than a confidence in it.

All the enemies of God will forever suffer untold misery under His mighty hand. They may resist His law, but they cannot resist His punishment. Two attributes of God will shine in hell: wrath and power. "What if God, willing to show his wrath, and to make his power known, endured with much longsuffering the vessels of wrath fitted to destruction" (Rom. 9:22). If a man cannot escape earthly death, how shall he escape the second death? And how great must that vengeance be that is backed by omnipotence! May every sinner who reads this page carefully consider the futility of rebelling against the Almighty!

Comfort

An ocean of comfort is here for believers. God's power gives action to all His attributes. How empty would we be if God had said, "I am true, wise, loving and righteous but not powerful"! Instead, God's power comforts us in all afflictions and distresses. Even our Savior, while on the cross, seeing His Father's frown, exercised faith in the Father's power, calling Him *Eli*, a title that designates His power. This attribute comforts us in all corruptions and temptations. No enemy without or within is so strong that He cannot conquer it. God is not lacking for power to accomplish all that He has promised. Once He has willed a thing, it cannot but come to pass. His power enables us to persevere in the faith. Our Lord said, "My Father, which gave them me, is greater than all; and no man is able to pluck them out of my Father's hand" (John 10:29). We "are kept by the power of God" (1 Peter 1:5). When the cause of God in the earth seems feeble and desperate, here is cause for comfort: God can raise the dead. He need only say the word, and His enemies will fall. "By the breath of his nostrils are they consumed" (Job 4:9). He turns night into day very quickly. Revelation 18 tells of Babylon falling in one day. But we must remember that God usually waits to act until we have felt our extremity and exhausted our own resources so that His power might be more conspicuous and admirable. Our lowest ebbs are but scenes for the brightest display of His power. Let saints under trial take courage!

Exhortation

Let us bring our minds to think much and often on this attribute. Our fears will disappear in view of it. A right knowledge of this truth is essential to all true religion. Without it, we cannot pray aright nor love nor fear God aright. Our experience will be more stable if we only remember that God is almighty.

Let us trust God increasingly. His power renders Him worthy of our deepest confidence. "Trust ye in the LORD for ever: for in the LORD JEHOVAH is everlasting strength" (Isa. 26:4). God's power was especially in view by Abraham. "And being fully persuaded that, what he had promised, he was able also to perform" (Rom. 4:21). We have even more reason to trust Him than did the Old Testament patriarchs, seeing we have so many clearer evidences of His power in the person and work of Christ. This attribute should produce fear in the wicked, and so should it produce in the righteous trust. It empowers God's mercy and goodness toward us. Sometimes God's power is the only thing we can trust, like the three Hebrews who declared, "Our God whom we serve is able to deliver us from the burning fiery furnace" (Dan. 3:17). There can be no trust in God without an eye to His power.

Let us learn humility and submission. "Humble yourselves therefore under the mighty hand of God" (1 Peter 5:6). What folly to resist infinite power!

Let us learn not to fear man. Would you fear a dwarf if you had a giant to guard you? Surely the fear of man is an insult to God, before whom "the nations are as a drop of a bucket, and are counted as the small dust of the balance" (Isa. 40:15).

Let us therefore fear the Lord God. "Sanctify the LORD of hosts himself; and let him be your fear, and let him be your dread" (Isa. 8:13). He can make a hair or a crumb to strangle us. He can turn sweet morsels into bitter. He can make our conscience a devouring lion. He can conquer every empire as if none opposed. We should stand in awe of that power that can destroy us. We are to fear Him because He can, but bless Him because, according to His goodness in Christ, He will not.

11

THE HOLINESS OF GOD

One of the loftiest descriptions of the majesty and excellence of
God is found in the song sung by Moses and the children of Israel
after the Red Sea victory. "Who is like unto thee, O Lord, among
the gods? who is like thee, glorious in holiness, fearful in praises, doing wonders?" (Ex. 15:11). The holiness of God is His glory, as His
grace is His riches. A God with the least degree of unholiness would
be a monster, more a devil than a God.

This attribute seems to have an excellence above the other perfections of God. It is the only one that is repeated three times both
in the Old Testament and in the New. "Holy, holy, holy, is the Lord
of hosts: the whole earth is full of his glory" (Isa. 6:3). "Holy, holy,
holy, Lord God Almighty, which was, and is, and is to come" (Rev.
4:8). God singles it out to swear by, as if it were the dearest to Him.
"Once have I sworn by my holiness that I will not lie unto David"
(Ps. 89:35). "The Lord God hath sworn by his holiness" (Amos 4:2).
No other attribute could give an assurance parallel to it. Holiness is
God's glory and beauty. It is His very life, for He swears both by His
life and by His holiness. How often He swears, "As I live, saith the
Lord." Holiness is the crown and beauty of all His other perfections.
His power is a holy power. His wisdom is a holy wisdom. Without
holiness, His patience would be an indulgence, His mercy fond-
ness, His wrath madness, His power tyranny, and His wisdom mere
subtlety. His name, which stands for all He is, is holy (Ps. 103:1).
"Holy is his name" (Luke 1:49). All His actions are performed in
holiness. "The Lord is holy in all his works" (Ps. 145:17).

The Nature of God's Holiness

Generally speaking, holiness is a perfect and unpolluted freedom from all evil. It is moral rectitude and integrity. God acts in a way becoming to His own excellence. More specifically, we mark the following points.

Holiness is essential to God's nature. Apart from it, He would not be God. He did not choose to be holy, for then He might have chosen to be unholy as well. Nor was He somehow compelled to be holy. Rather, holiness is a free necessity. It is simply inconceivable that He should be anything but holy.

God alone is absolutely holy. "There is none holy as the LORD" (1 Sam. 2:2). "Who shall not fear thee, O Lord, and glorify thy name? for thou only art holy" (Rev. 15:4). No creature can be absolutely holy because all creatures are mutable. Any holiness in us derives from Him and is all of grace. Even sinless angels are said to be charged with folly by God (Job 4:18) because their holiness is finite and is separate from their essence, but God's is infinite and essential.

God perfectly hates all evil, inasmuch as He also loves that which is just. He is pleased with the good things He brings forth on the occasion of sin, but this pleasure is in His own goodness and wisdom rather than in the sinful act. Since evil is the opposite of holiness, God must of necessity hate it. If He did not, He would hate Himself and become an enemy to His own nature. Furthermore, He hates evil intensely. It is abhorrent to Him. He hates the very workers of iniquity because of their sinful nature (Ps. 5:5). His anger is as infinite as His love and mercy and is as much a perfection as they are. God hates evil wherever it is found. He sometimes punishes the sins of His redeemed ones more than those of others in this life. We read of no lost souls who had to endure the fish's belly like the prophet Jonah. Christ rebuked the Pharisees as children of the devil, but He did not call any of them Satan, as He did Simon

Peter (Matt. 16:23). God hates evil perpetually, without interruption. He "is angry with the wicked every day" (Ps. 7:11). God may be reconciled to the sinner but never to the sin. His reconciliation to the sinner takes place only because of His putting away of the sin by Christ.

God is so holy that He cannot but love holiness in others. "The righteous LORD loveth righteousness" (Ps. 11:7). He is not indebted to any of His creatures for their righteousness. Rather, they are indebted to Him. But God does love the stamp He himself puts on a person.

God is so holy that He cannot positively will or encourage sin in anyone. There is no contradiction in God. Holiness cannot be the cause of unholiness. Thus, we read in James 1:13 that God does not tempt any man to sin. Nor does He command anyone to sin. Nor does He secretly inspire any evil into anyone, for He is "a God of truth and without iniquity, just and right is he" (Deut. 32:4). Nor does God coerce man to sin. Sin is a voluntary act on the part of the wicked. Of course, this in no way diminishes God's absolute sovereignty; it simply clears God of any complicity in sin. How could He excite us to that which, when it is done, He will be sure to condemn? If God were the author of sin, why should our consciences accuse us? "Is there unrighteousness with God? God forbid" (Rom. 9:14).

God cannot do any evil Himself. There is no defect in God's holiness. There is no variableness with Him (James 1:17).

The Demonstration of God's Holiness

First, we see God's holiness in the original state of creation. The first estate of the angels was holy (Jude 6). The first estate of man was likewise holy. "God hath made man upright" (Eccl. 7:29). Man was made in God's moral image, which is one of "righteousness and true holiness" (Col. 3:10; Eph. 4:24). The clearness of the stream points to the purity of the fountain.

Second, we see God's holiness in His work as lawgiver and judge. All His laws and administration of justice reflect the rectitude of His nature. Moses asked Israel, "What nation is there so great, that hath statutes and judgments so righteous as all this law, which I set before you this day?" (Deut. 4:8).

1. The moral law points to the holiness of God. "The law is holy, and the commandment holy, and just, and good" (Rom. 7:12). "The law of the LORD is perfect" (Ps. 19:7). God's law enjoins all good and disowns all evil, not merely for the benefit of the man himself as the doer of deeds or merely for the benefit of mankind as recipients of the deeds but because the law of God is holy in its own character, considered in itself. Man's laws are concerned only with outward behavior, but God's law is concerned with the heart and attitude. "The law is spiritual" (Rom. 7:14). It commands not only a front porch free of mud but also a closet free of cobwebs. Even God Himself will not violate this holy law, for that would make Him an enemy to Himself. He would sooner expose His Son to shame and death than to pardon the guilty in a manner that violates His standard of holiness and justice.

2. The ceremonial law points to the holiness of God. The people of Israel, daily if not hourly, witnessed reminders of God's holy character in the Levitical sacrifices, washings, ordinances, dietary laws, and the like.

3. God revealed His holiness in the promises and threats annexed to His law. Sin is rendered odious and destructive, while righteousness is commended and promoted. The end of the threatening was to instill fear in men and deter them from evil. The end of the promises was to instill hope in men and direct them to obedience. "Having therefore these promises, dearly beloved, let us cleanse ourselves

from all filthiness of the flesh and spirit, perfecting holiness in the fear of God" (2 Cor. 7:1).

4.   In holiness, God inflicts judgment upon those who violate His law. Divine holiness is the root of divine justice, and divine justice is the triumph of divine holiness. Both concepts are expressed in Scripture by one word: *righteousness*. The first thoughts that enter the mind of a man who sees a gallows or a guillotine are the heinousness of the crime and the righteousness of the judge. Thus, when we consider the casting out of once-glorious angels and the curse upon all mankind for one sin, we cannot but see God's holiness. Even the instruments used in committing sin are detestable to God. He pronounced a special curse upon the serpent, which was the tool of the devil. He forbade Israel to take the gold that the Canaanites had used in idolatry. "The graven images of their gods shall ye burn with fire: thou shalt not desire the silver or gold that is on them, nor take it unto thee, lest thou be snared therein: for it is an abomination to the LORD thy God" (Deut. 7:25). The earth itself was cursed for man's sake. Infants perished in the fire that rained on Sodom. Achan's family and herds were stoned with him. All these and many other events manifest the holiness of God.

Third, we see God's holiness in the restoration of man. The whole scene of redemption is nothing but a discovery of the holiness, righteousness, and justice of God. Consider the way this redemption is accomplished. Nothing shows God's holy wrath like His punishing His own Son. Better that the Son of God should die than that sin should live. The Father did not diminish the wrath because His Son was the object of it; He gave the full measure. Infinite holiness allowed for no paternal leniency. It was as if God's affection for His holiness surmounted His affection for His Son. "It pleased the LORD to bruise Him" (Isa. 53:10). While Christ hung on the cross, the Father seemed to lay aside the heart of a father and put on the garb of an enemy. This was only proper since Christ put on the garb of a sinner. The death of Christ vindicated the honor of God. It restored the credit of divine holiness in the world by destroying sin and restoring the image of God in man. Therefore, the Father raised up the Son from the grave and exalted Him in the highest. "Thou hast loved righteousness, and hated iniquity; therefore God, even thy God, hath anointed thee with the oil of gladness above thy fellows" (Heb. 1:9). Ultimately, God seems to value His holy hatred of sin above any other attribute. Mercy and grace were not allowed to be shown unless holy wrath be shown. God will not show mercy at the expense of justice.

We further see God's holiness in the conditions He requires for justification—namely, repentance and faith. We must condemn our own righteousness and disown all that we own. We must cling by faith to His righteousness—that is, the righteousness He appoints and accepts and has wrought for us in the person of Christ. The whole design of redemption is to reinstate us in a resemblance to God's holiness. Regeneration and sanctification and final perfection are the happiness of God's people—to be holy as He is holy.

The Holiness of God in All His Dealings with Sin

We tread on dangerous ground here. We must not be too curious but, rather, willing not to know what God has seen fit to conceal from us. Nevertheless, we will lay out some propositions to defend God's character from charges of unholiness concerning the existence of sin.

First, God is not unholy for having created man in a mutable state. God made all He made in great wisdom, as we have already considered. It pleased Him to give man as a rational creature the liberty of choice. If he did obey, his obedience might be the more valuable; if he sinned, his sin would be the more inexcusable. God was under no obligation to make man immutable. In fact, no creature can be immutable because God only is immutable and infinitely perfect. No angel or man was forced to sin. They sinned willingly. In the words of the Preacher, "they sought out many inventions" (Eccl. 7:29). Though God did make man mutable, He did not create man in a sinful state but "very good" (Gen. 1:31). Adam had every reason not to sin. He had a natural tendency to obedience. He possessed God-given resources to resist all temptation. Nor did God cause him to fall. God did not offer the fruit to Eve. Also, it was she, not God, who took and ate and gave to Adam. The ruin of a house brought about by a careless tenant in no way reflects on the builder who left it in a good condition at the first.

Second, God is not unholy for giving man a law He knew man would not keep. The law was not above Adam's strength. In his original state, he could have kept it. Should an earthly magistrate forbear to make good laws because he knows some in his realm will not obey them? Now that man is fallen, God in holiness still maintains His law. Some people think this is unjust and that God should relax His law now that man cannot obey it. But must God leave His holiness because man left his? God's knowledge beforehand of all the actions of men in no way necessitates or causes those actions to occur. Man voluntarily runs into sin. God's prescience does not take away the liberty of man in his action.

Third, God is not unholy for having decreed the rejection of some men. Reprobation is a passing by of some who were considered as already wicked. Reprobation did not make them wicked. It is not a decree of a crime but of a punishment. God might have thus passed by the whole race and justly condemned us all to hell. He has the right to withhold His power as He pleases. Reprobation is not an action but a cessation of action, leaving man to himself. If a man is allowed to carry out his own desires, he cannot fault God for the trouble that ensues. Any other view makes God to be indebted some way to the creature, which robs Him of His Godhood.

Fourth, God is not unholy for allowing sin to enter the world. He did not properly will the existence of sin, but He willed not to hinder it. To say God wills sin as He does other things is to deny His holiness. On the other hand, to say sin entered without anything of God's will is to deny His omnipotence. He did not directly will sin; rather, He decreed not to give the grace necessary to prevent it. He cannot will evil as evil but as to bring forth a higher good according to His infinite wisdom. Though He does not approve of sin, He does approve of the act of His will whereby He permits sin. And He approves of the ultimate end He will accomplish—namely, the exaltation of Himself as the Savior of sinners. He could never be displeased with any of His decrees.

If anyone should still call the holiness of God into question due to His permission of sin, consider some additional arguments. Scripture itself speaks in terms of permission. God "in times past suffered all nations to walk in their own ways" (Acts 14:16). This permission was not a moral permission given to man so he might sin with impunity. But it was God's determination not to prevent an act He could have prevented. Remember, He did prevent Abimelech from sinning with Sarah: "I also withheld thee from sinning against me: therefore suffered I thee not to touch her" (Gen. 20:6). But He did not prevent Adam from sinning. He left Satan free to tempt and Adam free to resist. God is in no way the efficient cause of sin. Permission is not action, nor is it the cause of action. The person committing the action is the cause. Furthermore, God was under no obligation to hinder angels or man from sin. Though we speak of our being obligated to help the needy or avert disaster, this obligation lies upon us because of our natural ties as one common blood; we are our brother's keeper. But these ties do not apply to God. He was no more obligated to prevent sin than He was obligated to create us in the first place. Having given Adam the strength to resist temptation, God was under no obligation to extend further grace. Grace is never a matter of debt! Under the arrangements then in place, even if Adam had prayed to God for preservation from sin, God would have been under no obligation to give it. He had already done enough for him and did not act unjustly in leaving him to the principles of his nature.

Having cleared God's name of any unholiness in the existence of evil, it is noteworthy that He prevents more sin than He permits. The hedges of sin are larger than the outlets. The psalmist declares, "Surely the wrath of man shall praise thee: the remainder of wrath shalt thou restrain" (86:10). If God did not limit sin, the world would at once descend into a public stew, a lake of Sodom, a slaughterhouse of murder. Also, we must always keep in mind that God permitted sin in order to accomplish a greater good. Only by the entrance of sin could we have ever seen the wonders of saving mercy. Furthermore, the justice of God revealed in the punishment of the wicked would have remained an unknown perfection.

Fifth, God is not unholy when He sustains the life of sinners. All creatures depend on God for their every faculty. Nothing lives, moves, or has being apart from Him. But God instills no evil in His creatures. He enables us to act, but the moral goodness or badness of our action is determined by the object, circumstances, and motive of the act. No action in itself is evil. For example, eating is good, if it be food justly obtained and eaten in moderation with thanksgiving to God. But eating is evil if it be an act of rebellion, as did Adam. Nevertheless, God was not implicated in Adam's sin merely because He gave him the hand to hold the fruit and the mouth to eat it. Or consider this example: the taking of human life is evil if it be with malice or any sinful motive, but it is good if it be in administering justice or in fighting a just war. Therefore, we must distinguish between the substance of any act and the sinfulness of the act. Sin may cleave to an act like leprosy to an arm, but the arm itself is not the problem. The soil, rain, and sunshine should not be blamed for the poison that some plants produce, for these same things also nourish plants that bear good food. The nature of the plant is the real issue.

Even so, the nature of man is what produces sin, not the God who gives the man his life. Blotches of ink on the page must be attributed to a broken pen, not to the hand that does the writing. The clock that keeps poor time is no reflection against the one who winds it each day. Certainly, God could annihilate fallen man, but He is more pleased to govern him in keeping with his nature as a rational yet fallen creature. Though man has an evil end in view as he acts, God has a good end in view in allowing those same acts. Joseph's brothers intended to destroy him, but God intended to preserve both him and them, and He accomplished His purpose even as they thought to accomplish theirs. "Ye thought evil against me; but God meant it unto good" (Gen. 50:20). God concurred with Satan in spoiling Job but to very different ends: Satan thought to make Job curse God, but God thought to make Job worship Him. Judas thought to satisfy his covetousness at Christ's expense, but God thought to satisfy His justice and manifest His love at Christ's expense.

Sixth, God is not unholy when He provides the objects man uses in sin. God placed the tree of the knowledge of good and evil in the midst of the garden, but it had no internal influence on Adam's will. The tree could not force itself on Adam. Objects that in themselves are good may be employed by man in sinful schemes. For example, riches are used by some to their advantage and to the advantage of others, but they are also used selfishly by others to their detriment. God's character is not blemished by the fact that He places these objects before man that will be used sinfully. God has the right to use the corruptions of man for His divine purposes. He can use His creatures with whatever nature they possess, according to His will. Since the seeds of all sin are in every man's nature, God has the right to hinder the sprouting of some seeds and allow others to grow, and to remove some objects man may use to sin and offer other objects to accomplish His desired end.

Seventh, God is not unholy by withdrawing common grace from a sinful creature, whereby he falls into more sin. God gave grace to Eli to reprove his sons for their sins, but He did not give grace to those sons to pay heed. "They hearkened not unto the voice of their father, because the LORD would slay them" (1 Sam. 2:25). When Scripture speaks of God's hardening of a man's heart, it refers not to a positive action upon that man but to leaving that man to his own hardness, even though it was in God's power to soften, quicken, and change him. God hardens men by not removing the incentives to sin, by not curbing the desires ready to comply with those incentives, by not causing admonitions to be effectual, by not convicting their consciences as He had previously done. Thus, we read, "God also gave them up to uncleanness through the lusts of their own hearts" (Rom. 1:24). While God's withdrawing of grace may be considered the logical cause, it is not the true and natural cause. Man's wicked heart is the cause of any increase in sin. In this way, both God and Pharaoh are said to have hardened Pharaoh's heart (Ex. 7:13; 8:32). But in none of this is God the real cause of man's first or subsequent sin, any more than the withholding of the sun is the cause of darkness. Therefore, God is guilty of no crime by ceasing to hold back the sin that seeks to break out from within the man. Moreover, God does not withdraw from man until man withdraws from Him. In Adam, we have all provoked Him. Would anyone blame a father who, after repeated counsels and corrections, leaves his wayward son to his own devices and withdraws the assistance he rejected and scoffed at? Is God obligated to continue His grace once it is spurned? No, for grace knows no obligation; otherwise, grace is no longer grace. God may extend it or withhold it as He pleases. If we demand what is due to us, we might as well demand our further misery and punishment, for that is what God is obligated to give us.

Eighth, God is not unholy for commanding things that seem to be against nature or in conflict with His precepts. For example, He told Abraham to offer up Isaac as a sacrifice. He told the Israelites to "borrow" the jewels from the Egyptians. He even made the Egyptians willing to "lend" (Ex. 11:2-3; 12:36). Quite simply, God's authority overrides all private and public authority whatsoever. He who is the lawgiver may dispose with His own law as He pleases. As creator and owner of all, He may do with His property as He wishes. He cannot command anyone to commit sin, but He can dispose of the lives and goods of His creatures in any way He sees fit.

Now let us mark what we should learn from this attribute.

Instruction and Information

Mankind despises this attribute of God more than any other. Man-made deities possess various qualities but never this perfection. We would rather have any kind of God except a holy one. It is a testimony to the evil of man's nature that this most glorious attribute is the most hated. All sin is especially against the holiness of God.

Let us mark some ways in which men hold this perfection in contempt:

❖ *By having unworthy thoughts of God in our minds.* Heathens ascribed to their gods the same sins and passions they themselves had, thereby hoping to find protection from their own sins. But how many professing Christians are just as guilty in that they fancy God as they wish He were, rather than how He truly is! Invariably the "new God" is less holy and more willing to wink at sin. "Thou thoughtest that I was altogether such an one as thyself" is God's accusation in Psalm 50:21.

❖ *By defacing the image of God in our own souls.* We were made in God's image, and so to give ourselves to sin is to slight our Maker. In the minds of many, being a real man means to be an ungodly, immoral wretch, equivalent to an incarnate devil.

❖ *By blaming God for our sin.* We all want some excuse for our sin, and this is the ultimate excuse—"God was an accessory to my crime." Adam said as much, "The woman whom thou gavest to be with me, she gave me of the tree, and I did eat" (Gen. 3:12).

❖ *By twisting Scripture to find a shelter for our sin.* How much debauchery and drunkenness have men defended by verses like Ecclesiastes 2:24, "There is nothing better for a man, than that he should eat and drink, and that he should make his soul enjoy good," making God's Word an encouragement to sin! Or Matthew 5:11, "Not that which goeth into the mouth defileth a man."

❖ *By praying to God to help us in our sin.* Some thieves have been known to always pray for the success of their robbery. Some covetous men ask God for more unjust gain. All this is to pretend that God is a friend to crime rather than to pray as we ought, "Hallowed [i.e., holy] be thy name."

❖ *By scoffing at holiness in true Christians.* A Christian's holiness is partial. Those who scoff at partial holiness do all the more despise perfect holiness in God. The rebel who cannot injure the king personally often injures the king's loyal subjects who are nearby.

❖ *By carelessly approaching God in worship,* without due preparation and cleansing of our hearts from all known sin. A holy God deserves holy worship and holy worshipers. Coming with our sin is like Aaron the priest presenting a bucket of dung in the most holy place as a sacrifice to God.

❖ *By depending on self-righteousness to please God.* Men imagine that God can be satisfied with such a pitiful little—a few mumbled prayers and outward rituals, or perhaps building a hospital! "I have peace offerings with me; this day have I payed my vows," says the wicked woman of Proverbs 7:14, as she returns to her adultery.

❖ *By complaining that God's law is too strict.* This is the same as wishing God were as defiled as we are. It amounts to blaming God for consulting with His own righteousness and codifying it. Behind this is a desire to sin with impunity.

❖ *By adding vain opinions to Holy Scripture.* The Catholic Church does this with the teaching concerning venial sins—that is, those sins that are not so unholy, which deserve to be pardoned more than punished. But the truth is this: "Cursed is every one that continueth not in all things which are written in the book of the law to do them" (Gal. 3:10). Also, there is the Romanist teaching concerning works of supererogation—that is, works that God has not required, which bring merit to the doers and to others as well. Thus, they whip their bodies and wear rough clothing. Even the Jews who despised the holiness of God never dreamed of such perversion as this. This teaching assumes that God's law is not sufficient and man can surpass God's standard of holiness. Thus, those who are bankrupt themselves pretend to have enough to loan to their neighbors.

Our fall from God is exceedingly great. The distance between God and us is no less than the distance between God and Satan. In Adam, we stripped off that holiness that was the glory of our nature and our only means of glorifying God. Let none imagine that the fall was a slight tripping!

All unholiness is against the nature of God. "Thou art of purer eyes than to behold evil, and canst not look on iniquity" (Hab. 1:13). Sin is spoken of in the vilest terms: it is the abominable thing that God hates, the vomit of a dog, a putrefying carcass in an open grave, and stinking excrement (Jer. 44:4; 2 Peter 2:22; Rom. 3:13; Phil. 3:8). We must hate it if we love God. "Ye that love the Lord hate evil" (Ps. 97:10).

No unholiness will escape God's punishment. His hatred of sin must be manifested. His holiness demands it; otherwise, He would deny His own essence. His threats to punish are not empty. If a way is not found to separate the sin from the sinner, then the sinner must be punished forever. How can God hate the sin and love the one who commits it when the natures of the two parties are so opposed to Him? Sinful men assume God must hate Himself in order to have communion with them.

If any sinners were to be saved, God's holiness had to be satisfied by a sufficient mediator. The law could not be abolished to pardon the guilty. God could not change His holiness to accommodate man's unholiness. If God justifies the guilty, He must do it in a way that maintains justice. The atonement by Christ was the only way to display at once the holiness and the mercy of God. In the gospel, God is both "just and the justifier of him which believeth in Jesus" (Rom. 3:26).

There can be no justification of a sinner by anything in himself. After sin set foot in the world, man had nothing left to offer God. At that point, our plea could only be "Enter not into judgment with thy servant: for in thy sight shall no man living be justified" (Ps. 143:2) and "Woe is me! for I am undone" (Isa. 6:5). But God set forth a righteousness, wrought by the incarnate Son of God, which answers perfectly to the holiness of God.

The deity of Christ may be argued by this attribute. He is called "the Holy One" (Acts 2:27; 3:14). John by inspiration indicates that the cry of the seraphim in Isaiah 6:3, "Holy, holy, holy," had reference to God the Son (John 12:37–41).

God's holiness makes Him fit to govern the world. The Apostle asks, "If God be unrighteous, how shall He judge the world?" (Rom. 3:5–6). As omniscience makes Him fit to be a judge, holiness makes Him fit to be a righteous judge.

Christianity is of divine origin. It is the only true religion, for it reveals a holy God and makes men holy like Him. It is a "doctrine which is according to godliness" (1 Tim. 6:3). God bids us, "Be ye holy; for I am holy" (1 Peter 1:16).

Comfort

Though bitter to a lost soul, this doctrine is sweet to the saint. "My heart rejoiceth in the LORD. . . . There is none holy as the LORD (1 Sam. 2:1–2). "My spirit hath rejoiced in God my Savior . . . and holy is his name" (Luke 1:47, 49).

By God's covenant mercy, believers have a share in this attribute. He makes us to be "partakers of his holiness" (Heb. 12:10). What comfort would it be if He made us unholy?

God is a fit object of our trust. Who could possibly trust an unholy God? We might well fear that His power would crush us, His mercy overlook us, or His wisdom design against us, were it not for this attribute of holiness. But God swears by His holiness (Ps. 89:35), laying it as a pawn for the security of His promise. On the grounds of His holiness, we pray. "If ye then, being evil, know how to give good gifts unto your children, how much more shall your Father which is in heaven give good things to them that ask him?" (Matt. 7:11). We can come to Him in our distress and find help that is good help indeed. We can depend on Him to keep His promises to protect and preserve us, for His holiness will not allow Him to violate His covenant with us in Christ.

God highly values that which is holy. Nothing is more precious in heaven than what is most like God in holiness. "The LORD hath set apart him that is godly for himself" (Ps. 4:3). Believers find comfort in being "partakers of the divine nature, having escaped . . . corruption" (2 Peter 1:4). If God delights in us now, think how pleasing we will be to Him in our sinlessly glorified state!

God will not leave the work of redemption in us unfinished. "Being confident of this very thing, that he which hath begun a good work in you will perform it until the day of Jesus Christ" (Phil. 1:6). Therefore, with David we can confidently pray, "Preserve my soul; for I am holy" (Ps. 86:2). It is God's purpose to sanctify His church and "present it to himself a glorious church, not having spot, or wrinkle, or any such thing; but that it should be holy and without blemish" (Eph. 5:26–27), and He will not cease to purify us until He can say, "Thou art all fair, my love; there is no spot in thee" (Song 4:7).

Exhortation

Let us get and maintain a strong apprehension of this attribute. Without it we can never exalt God in our hearts.

It will convict us of our sin. Our depth of conviction is proportionate to our sense of God's holiness.

It will keep us humble, no matter how holy we are. Even sinless angels hide their faces from infinite Holiness. The holiest of men is detestable to himself.

It will make us approach God more reverently and heartily. "Holy and reverend is his name" (Ps. 111:9). A growing sense of His holiness will prompt us to our duties with deeper fervency.

It will keep us from sin by producing a greater fear of God in us. A man tends to become like the God he worships. Little wonder that the heathen were full of vices and lusts, since their gods were of the same character. But the true and living God is pure and righteous, and it becomes us to fling away all our idols, mortify every lust, and be on guard against every temptation.

It will make us eager to be conformed to God's image. A good example stimulates an admirer to imitation. Here is the supreme example that challenges every regenerate heart to model Him. "But we all, with open face beholding as in a glass the glory of the Lord, are changed into the same image from glory to glory, even as by the Spirit of the Lord" (2 Cor. 3:18).

It will make us patient and content under all God's providences. As a king, He governs His subjects with perfect justice. Our Savior, in His time of sharpest agony and humiliation, adored the holiness of the Father. "O my God, I cry in the daytime, but thou hearest not; and in the night season, and am not silent. But thou art holy" (Ps. 22:2-3). It is as if He said, "I find no fault in your dealings. You are holy in all you do." God melts us down like gold so we might receive the impression of His grace. All His dealings with us are in holiness and for our holiness.

Let us honor and glorify this attribute in God's nature. Every creature is indebted to worship God on account of His holiness. "Let them praise thy great and terrible name; for it is holy" (Ps. 99:3). In honoring God's holiness, we honor all His other perfections.

We exalt this attribute *by making it the ground of our love to God.* That which renders God amiable to Himself should render Him lovely to us also. We should not love Him for purely selfish reasons but for His essential beauty.

We exalt this attribute *by recognizing that holiness is behind every temporal judgment in the world.* His severe treatment of His enemies here is but the breath of His holiness.

We exalt this attribute *by taking notice of His every fulfilled promise and His every act of mercy.* His faithfulness to His covenant people calls for praise and thanksgiving.

We exalt this attribute *by trusting His covenant and promise despite outward appearances to the contrary.*

We exalt this attribute *by showing a greater love for holiness when others are despising it*. Let us say with the psalmist, "They have made void thy law. Therefore I love thy commandments above gold" (119:126–127). If we honor Him by acknowledging His holiness, He will honor us by communicating it to us. "Them that honor me I will honor" (1 Sam. 2:30).

Let us labor after conformity to God in this most excellent perfection. The purity of our Lord should move us to purify ourselves. "And every man that hath this hope in him purifieth himself, even as he is pure" (1 John 3:3). Though a creature can never equal the Creator in holiness, we should have the same kind of holiness. Adam wanted to be like God in knowledge, but he should have aspired to be like God in holiness.

Truly God is our pattern in holiness. His precept instructs us more, but His example affects us more. Conformity to His image consists in an imitation of His law, which is the transcript of His holiness and an imitation of His Christ, who is the image of His holiness. As He died on the cross, so we die to sin; as He rose from the grave, we rise from our lusts; as He ascended on high, our affections ascend to heavenly things.

It is only in moral perfection that we are commanded to be like God. No creature has a capacity for more than that. The demons are nearer to Him in strength and knowledge than we are, but they are far from His holiness. Our chief manner of glorifying God is not to applaud His purity but to conform to it. When God commands us, "Sanctify the LORD of hosts himself; and let him be your fear, and let him be your dread (Isa. 8:13), He is saying, "Manifest the purity of my nature by the holiness of your lives." We must keep up God's reputation in the world.

Holiness is our beauty. The beauty of every copied thing is its likeness to the original—not so much being merely the work of God but having His moral stamp upon us. Holiness is our life. The life of our soul, which is our primary part, consists not in its existence but in its moral operations. What life is to the body, holiness is to the soul. Without holiness, we are dead. Holiness makes us fit for communion with God. Without it, "no man shall see the Lord" (Heb. 12:14). God and man cannot enjoy each other unless they resemble each other. Also, holiness is the evidence of our election and adoption by God. He chose us in Christ "before the foundation of the world, that we should be holy" (Eph. 1:4). He will not own us as His children without this mark upon us.

Therefore, let us study the holiness of Christ. Occasional glances will not suffice. Let us engage our hearts in love to God for His holiness. Let us make God our end, and we shall find by degrees a silent likeness passing upon us and within us. Let us make God's holiness our pattern in every deliberate act. If we do these things, how happy we shall be!

Let us labor to strengthen the areas of weakness and always be growing in holiness. The more we are like God, the more we enjoy Him. "He that hath my commandments, and keepeth them, he it is that loveth me: and he that loveth me shall be loved of my Father, and I will love him, and will manifest myself to him" (John 14:21).

Let us behave in a godly manner in all our approaches to God. "Holiness becometh thine house, O LORD, for ever" (Ps. 93:5). With Moses, we must remove our shoes, which figure speaks of putting off any defilement.

Let us woo God for holiness, for He alone is the source. "I am the LORD which sanctify you" (Lev. 20:8). Holiness is His favorite attribute, and He delights to impart it. Without Him, we cannot attain nor maintain it. But we must be content to have it by small measures and degrees. "And the very God of peace sanctify you wholly" (1 Thess. 5:23).

12

The Goodness of God

To the rich young ruler, our Lord asked, "Why callest thou me good? There is none good but one, that is, God" (Mark 10:18). God alone is essentially and perfectly good. This grand statement shows the futility of works-righteousness. None of us is naturally good. What could we possibly do to impress God? Those who attempt it would like to make God indebted to them. Man is ready to transform even faith into a work of merit and thus deny this plain statement of Christ's. Even our faith is not original to ourselves but is a gift from God. He is the source of all good.

The notion of goodness is inseparable from the notion of a God. He is not God if He is not good. "Truly God is good to Israel" (Ps. 73:1). "The Lord, The Lord God, merciful and gracious, long-suffering, and abundant in goodness" (Ex. 34:6).

What This Goodness Is

We are not referring to God's essential perfection or holiness or to His own blessedness or fullness in Himself. We are not referring even to His mercy, for goodness extends beyond mercy. Mercy pre-supposes a miserable object, but goodness needs no object at all. For example, creation was an act of goodness but not of mercy.

Rather, we are referring to the bounty of God, His charitableness and liberality in His management of all things. God is benevolent to all His creatures as creatures. This is the most pleasant perfection of God's nature, rendering Him lovely and desirable to us.

God's goodness comprehends all His attributes. When God would reveal Himself to Moses in the fullest manner a mortal could bear, He said, "I will make all my goodness pass before thee" (Ex. 33:19), as if goodness were the fountain of all the other streams of His glory. This is the captain attribute that leads the rest to act.

The Nature of God's Goodness

God is good by His own essence. He is more than good *in* His own essence, for all He created is good in that sense. But He is good *by* His own essence, in that none other causes Him to be good. Goodness is not a quality in Him but is His very nature. It is not a habit added to His essence but is His essence itself. His goodness is original, infinite, unlimited, eternal, and abundant.

God is the prime and chief goodness. All goodness in creatures derives from Him: "Thou art my Lord: my goodness extendeth not to thee" (Ps. 16:2). Our goodness is mutable, but His is immutable. He is the standard of goodness; nothing is good except as it resembles Him. There is no speck of evil in God. He is all good.

God's goodness is communicative. It is the very nature of goodness to be diffusive, to distribute. God is not envious of His goodness or stingy with it. He is more prone to communicate His goodness than is the sun to spread its rays and heat.

God is necessarily good. He is good by nature, not only by will. He could not have chosen to be bad. He is goodness itself and cannot act against His own nature. He did not have to create the world, but having chosen to do so, He had to make the world good.

Nevertheless, God is also freely good. The necessity of His goodness does not hinder the liberty of His actions. He is free in the communications of His goodness. He voluntarily exercises His goodness in that He chooses which good, or which degree of good, to do. He is under no constraint with regard to His goodness.

God delights in communicating His goodness. His pleasure in bestowing is greater than our pleasure in receiving. He does not hoard up His treasures as if He were envious of them. Rather, He rejoices to impart His riches. He delights to be petitioned by men for His goodness, and He seems eager to bestow good things to those who ask.

The display of goodness was the motive and end of all God's works of creation and providence. His motive and end must be in Himself, for nothing is higher than He. Therefore, this most amiable perfection claims the best right to be foremost displayed. In creating, God did not increase His excellence, but He did manifest it. Had He not created the world, He would have been unknown to any but Himself; but He produced creatures so that He might be known. The acknowledging of His goodness must be the great motive and end of all His works.

God Is Good

The better a person is, the more charitable he is. God is the best and most bountiful person, for there is none above Him. Since "every creature of God is good" (1 Tim. 4:4), and creatures derive their goodness from their Creator, He must be the best, the supreme good. As the cause is richer than the effect, He must be infinite goodness. Lest any should doubt God's goodness, let us defend it from two assaults.

First, God's goodness is not impaired by His allowing sin to enter the world. God in goodness created man with a capacity for happiness. Would it have been goodness if He had forced man to be happy against his will? God in goodness furnished Adam with a power to stand, and in goodness He left him free to use that power. Only with a freedom of choice would obedience have been obedience. God's goodness is no less goodness because man made ill use of it. It was man, not God, who fell. Furthermore, in goodness God allowed the fall of mankind so that He might show greater stores of His glory in redemption.

Second, God's goodness is not impaired by His discrimination as to the objects of it. God does not distribute His goodness equally; some things receive more of it than others. He did not make all things equally good, yet He made nothing evil. He is good to all, but not in the same degree. God's goodness to creatures is measured by their distinct usefulness to the common end. The faculty of the mind is better than that of speech, but speech is good in that it communicates what is in the mind. The inequality of God's goodness shows His goodness more than equality would. For example, it provides us with links in human society—the poor and the wealthy need each other. It provides reason both to praise and to petition God. Not all creatures have the same capacity in their natures for goodness. Man has a higher capacity than, say, birds, but this implies no fault in God's goodness. If God showed all His goodness to any creature, it would not be able to stand it: no man can see God and live (Ex. 33:20). God has the right to manifest His goodness according to His sovereign pleasure. He is the Lord of His gifts. If He pardons many rebels, must He therefore pardon them all? Is God less good because He will not distribute His goodness to those who despise Him and do not seek His favor? Is He not free to act according to His wise will and not according to man's faulty whims?

Moreover, God's punishing of evildoers in no way violates His goodness. Whatever God does is good, whether it be pleasant or painful to the creature. Punishment is not a moral evil in the person that inflicts it. Not punishing the wicked would be bad, not good. The justice of God is a part of His goodness. Goodness without justice would be impotent indulgence and would encourage rebellion and confusion. Could God be accounted good if He had the same attitude toward both evil and righteousness? Making and enforcing laws is part of God's goodness, inasmuch as it promotes goodness and restrains evil. "The law is holy, and the commandment holy, and just, and good" (Rom. 7:12). Law is no longer law without a penalty. It would be a perversion of goodness not to enforce the law. It would be a weak indulgence, not goodness, to bear forever with the unrepentant. "The LORD is known by the judgment which he executeth" (Ps. 9:16). How could it be good for God to see His goodness trampled upon and never vindicate His honor? If men turn God's goodness into a license to sin, God will turn His goodness into justice.

But punishment is not God's primary intention in giving the law. Otherwise, He would not hinder all the sin He does hinder. Punishment is called "his strange work" (Isa. 28:21). The primary purpose of the law is to encourage goodness in men. Divine goodness levels its hatred primarily on the sin, not on the sinner. The sinner falls under the punishment because his sin cleaves to him. But God in goodness often warns the sinner, giving him space to repent. When the punishment falls, it serves the good purpose of warning observers and future generations. For example, Christ told his audience to "remember Lot's wife" (Luke 17:32). Judgment is often mixed with mercy for the righteous. For example, the floodwaters that destroyed the world bore up the ark to the saving of Noah and his family. Some say that eternal punishment is against God's goodness, but how can God be good without punishing evil men as long as they continue evil in their nature? Must God be bad to His justice to be kind to His enemies? Is man better and kinder than God?

Finally, God's afflicting of His saints is no violation of His goodness. The believer's afflictions are for his good, for the increase of grace. Can we charge God with evil when the afflictions He sends His church serve to remove the dross, cure it of carelessness, increase its numbers, strengthen its graces, and provide opportunities to prove its love to its Savior? The prison epistles of Paul seem to have a higher strain than those he wrote while at liberty. It would be a want of goodness, or rather a mark of cruelty, for a father to leave his child without chastening. It is great goodness that makes us smart here instead of scorched hereafter.

The Manifestation of God's Goodness

First, we see God's goodness manifest in creation. According to the first chapter of Genesis, God's goodness was the prominent feature in creation, even more than His power. Seven times over, creation is described as *good*, thus reflecting the character of the Creator. If God had not been good, creation could not have been good. More than any other attribute, goodness was His stamp put upon everything. Creation was His first act of goodness outside Himself.

Every creature has some goodness about it by virtue of being created by a good God. "The Lord is good to all: and his tender mercies are over all his works" (Ps. 145:9). What a great display of goodness is it to give life to a fly! But let us concentrate on God's goodness to man in particular.

Our very body, with all its variety of members and beauty of proportion, testifies to God's goodness. It is a fit cabinet of clay to house the nobler faculty of the soul, which possesses excellent faculties of knowledge and discernment between good and evil. God made man in His own likeness of holiness. Had he not fallen into sin, man would have been as eternally happy as the angels. God in goodness made man to be a sort of link between the lower and the higher world, between earth and heaven. All this goodness was freely shown by God to man; God did not need us for anything. He did not have to create anything whatsoever, and He surely did not have to create such a good thing as man. What could be better than being made in God's image? Let us exclaim with the psalmist, "O Lord our Lord, how excellent is thy name in all the earth! . . . What is man, that thou art mindful of him?" (Ps. 8:1, 4).

Further consider all the conveniences God has freely provided for man. The world itself was made for mankind and given to him for his support and delight. God richly furnished the world for man with such things as light by which to see, air to breathe, and food for nourishment. Think of all the colors, fragrances, and tastes God in goodness gave to man in this beautiful mansion of earth! No doubt the garden of Eden was a model of the beauties and pleasures of another world.

God's goodness to man appears in the laws He gave and the covenant He made with him. The law was fitted to man's nature. Obedience was not above his reach. The precepts were easy and not grievous. They were suited to man's happiness and comfort. When man did sin, he went against all that was natural to him. In some texts, God seems more grieved for man's impairing his own happiness than for his violating divine authority: "O that thou hadst hearkened to my commandments! then had thy peace been as a river" (Isa. 48:18). God in goodness encouraged Adam to obedience by giving a threat for disobedience, which implied a promise for obedience. He could have simply acted as a sovereign and not given these incentives. But God seems to have valued the title of Benefactor above that of Lord, for He kindly solicits obedience from Adam. Even after the fall, God in goodness came to admonish him. "Hast thou eaten of the tree? . . . What is this that thou hast done?" (Gen. 3:11, 13). The promises and threats appeal to hope and fear, the two passions whereby man's nature is managed in this world. Since the reward implied to Adam was unmerited, this was especially an act of goodness on the part of God. As the death threatened was eternal, so was the life promised eternal. This eternal life was also a pure beam of divine goodness, for there was no proportion between Adam's obedience and such a great reward.

Second, we see God's goodness manifest in redemption. The whole gospel is nothing but one great mirror of God's goodness. "Good will toward men" was the summary of Christ's person and work given by the angels (Luke 2:14). Redemption originated in God's goodness. When man fell into sin, goodness would not stand by as a spectator but, by astonishing methods, would recover man from his deplorable calamity. God's great end was to demonstrate the liberality of His nature. He takes as a name for Himself the very term *love*, declaring in 1 John 4:8, "God is love." This goodness was undeserved. He who had no need to create us certainly had no need to redeem us. Far from meriting His goodness, mankind seems eager to put a stop to it. Yet above His tribunal of justice, God has erected a mercy seat. The Father, Son, and Spirit harmoniously function in the good work of accomplishing and applying redemption. This goodness extends beyond what we could ever imagine. No doubt Adam, after his sin, expected nothing from God but a curse, yet God also came with a promise. What more could we ask than what God's goodness has granted!

God's work of creation was an act of goodness, but the work of redemption shows even more goodness. In redemption, goodness must overcome justice. Creation only cost God some breath, but redemption cost the lifeblood of the incarnate Son of God. In redemption, God must overcome man's rebellion and unworthiness, neither of which were obstacles in creation.

God's goodness to man in redemption is greater than that shown to the angels. The confirming in holiness of the elect angels did not accrue from the work of the cross but was a sovereign appointment by God. It was for man that Christ died. As for the fallen angels, they were left to wallow in their sin forever. But to man, divine goodness holds out a hand drenched in blood for our rescue.

God's goodness to man in redemption is a greater goodness that even that which was manifested to Christ Himself for a season. In the familiar statement of John 3:16, the emphasis is upon the little word *so*, that is, upon the quality of God's love to sinners. He so loved the world, that He seemed for a time not to love His Son. He would rather spare us than Him. He would rather hear Him groan than us. He would rather have Him die than us. What higher manifestation of love could we ever conceive?

Now, let us mark some particular ways in which God's goodness in redemption appears.

1. It appears in God's very determination to save. We should not think that Christ's atonement secured the love of God for sinners but rather that God's love secured the atonement. Love was the first wheel in motion in salvation. "God commendeth his love toward us, in that, while we were yet sinners, Christ died for us" (Rom. 5:8). The words of Isaiah 32:8 apply to God Himself: "The liberal deviseth liberal things."

2. God's goodness in redemption appears in the gift of Christ. No better gift could be given even by God Himself. Here is a gift of infinite value. A million worlds could not compare to it. All the angels could not compare to it. This is the only begotten of the Father, His One and Only in whom He focused all of His delight. This Son He gave up to endure the frailties of human life, to be made a curse, to suffer and taste the bitter cup of death for a degenerate world. Even more, divine goodness raised up and exalted the Son, not only for Himself as the Redeemer, but for us as the redeemed. Thus, divine goodness centered in Him both in His cross and in His crown. We share in the merits of His humiliation as well as in the glories of His coronation. In giving us His Son, He gives us Himself. He is our God. In Christ, we inherit all things. What more could divine goodness do for us? What more could God give us than Himself?

3. God's goodness in redemption appears when we consider the sinful state of man. Man acted unreasonably in being discontented with God, and in joining in league with hell against Him. There was nothing in man to attract or allure God's love. A world of demerit and evil dwells in man. Every sin is infinite because it is against an infinite God. If he who hates his brother is a murderer to his brother (1 John 3:15), then he who hates God is a murderer to God. God had every right to abandon us in our utterly low condition. Furthermore, every generation continues to multiply provocations

against God, descending into idolatry and superstition, debasing the glory of God and reducing Him to the level of a mere animal. Man is powerless to change or improve himself. He is at peace with Satan. We would expect all God's perfections to unite against such rebels. Instead, God opens up a fountain of goodness, which swells above the heights of sin, and designs a Redeemer for us.

4. God's goodness in redemption appears in the exalted position to which He brings us. In Christ, human nature takes a higher dignity than it had in the original creation. Adam was called the son of God, but redeemed people are called the brothers of Christ. *He is not ashamed to call them brethren* (Heb. 2:11). We who were lower than the angels are elevated above them. What man sinfully aspired to, God in grace has more than granted. What more could God do to manifest His goodness?

5. God's goodness in redemption appears in the covenant of grace, which freed us from the covenant of works. Adam was created under a works covenant, but once broken, only the grace of God could condescend to arrange another covenant. If the first covenant with Adam was a stooping down on the part of God's sovereignty, the second covenant seems a stripping Himself of His majesty to show pure goodness. The first covenant was built on man's obedience; the second is built on God's inexpressible love and the obedience of Christ. The head of the first covenant was a mutable man; the head of the second is the immutable God-man. The covenant of grace imparts a new nature within a man. With Christ's perfect obedience for us, God accepts our personal obedience if it is sincere, even though imperfect. The second covenant is built on better promises than the first (Heb. 8:6). God gives Himself as the blessing of the covenant of grace. "God is not ashamed to be called their God" (Heb. 11:16), even though it might seem a disparagement to His majesty to give Himself to such unworthy people. He would rather show His goodness than His greatness. He stooped down as low as He could to satisfy our need. He even confirmed the covenant with

an oath lest we should doubt His goodness. Furthermore, He made faith the condition of this covenant—not perfect obedience on our part or exact knowledge but the easiest condition in its own nature, its only difficulty being man's pride and obstinacy. What could be easier than lifting up the eye to the brazen serpent to be cured of the fiery sting? Faith is also a most reasonable and necessary condition, for it is unthinkable that God should pardon the sinner and leave him to continue in rebellion.

6. God's goodness in redemption appears in His dealings with men to embrace this covenant. He does not raise armies like Mohammed to coerce outward compliance. Rather He gently and sweetly woos us with strong motions of affection to comply with His proposals. He appeals to us saying, "Come now, and let us reason together" (Isa. 1:18), and "Why will ye die, O house of Israel?" (Ezek. 33:11). How affectionately He invites sinners! His evangelists are ambassadors through whom He entreats His enemies to be reconciled to Him (2 Cor. 5:20). How readily does God receive men when they do turn to Him! Like the father in the parable, He runs to meet the returning prodigal son. "He delighteth in mercy" (Mic. 7:18). And how meltingly He bewails man's willing refusal of His mercy! "Oh that my people had hearkened unto me, and Israel had walked in my ways!" (Ps. 81:13). Though God has no human passions, the sincerity of His goodness can be communicated to us in no other terms than those with which we are familiar. There is no want of goodness in God's nature.

7. God's goodness in redemption appears in the ordinances He has instituted for the new covenant, especially the Lord's Supper. A feast with God is great; a feast on God is greater. The signs of the bruised and broken body and of the precious, sin-washing blood of the Lamb are given us for our refreshment. God's goodness complies with our senses and condescends to our weakness in giving us visible tokens of the Savior whom we cannot yet see with our bodily eyes. The blood of Christ was effectual to confirm the covenant of

grace by atoning for sinners. And in the Lord's Supper, we see the visible seal of that covenant. What else could Christ mean when He says, "This cup is the new testament [or covenant] in my blood, which is shed for you" (Luke 22:20)? God gave this ordinance to remind us of His goodness and faithfulness. When the Holy Spirit accompanies its observance, it is indeed a means of grace to our souls. In other words, it is a memorial, but it is more: when our hearts are engaged in it, we enjoy a special measure of communion with Christ. Inasmuch as the Gentiles by offering up sacrifices had fellowship with devils (1 Cor. 10:20), even so believers have fellowship with Christ by observing the Lord's Supper. What can we say for those who neglect this ordinance? They do show a low estimation of the goodness of God who appointed it.

Finally, we must note that in redemption, God restores us to a more excellent condition than Adam had originally. Jesus said, "I am come that they might have life, and that they might have it more abundantly" (John 10:10). Even our bodies will be in a higher state. Abundant goodness would have restored us to Adam's state, but superabundant goodness lifts us up to the very heights in a new heaven and a new earth. God's goodness in redemption even extends to the lower creation. Creation "itself also shall be delivered from the bondage of corruption into the glorious liberty of the children of God" (Rom. 8:21). All earthly creation was under Adam's dominion and was therefore cursed with him. But now, the second Adam accomplishes the "restitution of all things" (Acts 3:21). Thus, divine goodness spreads its triumph over all creation—the only exception being fallen angels, for whom there is no redemption for even so much as one.

Third, we see God's goodness manifest in providence. A mere man enjoys preserving what he fashions; how much more the great God who made all things good! The same goodness that created continues to operate in providential care for the creation. Let us mark some ways in which God's goodness in providence is evident:

1. It is evident in *the care God has for all creatures*. He cares not only for the higher forms of creation but for the very lowest as well. The psalmist proclaims, "The earth is full of thy riches" (Ps. 104:24). Every nook and cranny partakes of God's goodness. He preserves man and beast (Ps. 36:6). In the words of Paul at Lystra, "He did good, and gave us rain from heaven, and fruitful seasons, filling our hearts with food and gladness" (Acts 14:17). He protects His creatures from a thousand dangers of which we know nothing. He takes care of the animals, providing habitations and food. "That thou givest them they gather: thou openest thine hand, they are filled with good" (Ps. 104:28). He instructed Israel concerning the ox—to let him enjoy a Sabbath's rest and to eat as he works (Ex. 20:10; Deut. 25:4). If the ox was distressed on the Sabbath, it was to be delivered (Luke 14:5). God even threatened Israel with short-ness of life if they treated the birds cruelly (Deut. 22:6–7). He also cares for inanimate things, such as the flowers and the grass (Matt. 6:28–29). How low the Almighty bends to care for His creation! Moreover, He cares for the lowest of humanity. He gave orders to the masters not to abuse their slaves (Ex. 21:26–27). The poor were allowed to glean in the fields (Deut. 19:9–10). The criminal must not be given more than forty lashes (Deut. 25:3). Even the ungodly and unthankful, who deserve nothing but darkness and fire, enjoy the blessings of sunshine and rain (Matt. 5:45). In this sense, God "is the Saviour [or preserver] of all men" (1 Tim. 4:10).

2. God's goodness in providence is evident in *the preservation of human society*. In His power, He is able to do it, and in His good-ness, He is willing to do it. He accomplishes this through the giving of His moral law, the Ten Commandments, which address every person and every relationship. He has ordained human government, without which the world would be a den of wild beasts devouring each other. He restrains the internal passions of men, which human government is insufficient to curb. He equips people with various gifts by which to serve society as a whole. He sends judgments upon

sins that would annihilate society. How many wicked rulers have come to a bitter end! God especially enables murderers to be caught and brought to justice. For the present time it seems He is more patient with crimes against Himself than crimes against mankind. He even sometimes causes a man to act contrary to his natural passions and help his enemy in time of need. In some sense, God goes so far as to set aside His own right to govern, allowing the exercise of earthly authority for the sake of order, even though He could rightly claim the authority. For example, the father or husband in Israel had the right to override any vow made by his household (Num. 30:3–8).

3. God's goodness in providence is evident in that *He encourages anything of moral goodness in the earth*. Many times has He caused an Ahab to humble himself for a season, for the greater common good, even though the man's motives were selfish.

4. God's goodness in providence is evident in *providing His Holy Scripture*. The Bible we have is His word and rule. He has not left us without a recorded revelation of His mind and will. He has provided a roadmap for our journey. He has preserved it and made it to be translated into many languages, against the efforts of men and devils. Men wilder than beasts have been tamed by its power.

5. God's goodness in providence is evident in *the conversion of sinners*. Here His power and goodness unite. He breaks open the hardest of hearts with conviction of sin, reveals the excellence of Christ, and brings us to taste the sweetness of His blood. In goodness He called Saul of Tarsus but passed by his companions in travel. He is good in that He calls any when He is bound to call none. He delights in saving the lowest and the worst. "Not many wise men after the flesh, not many mighty, not many noble, are called" (1 Cor. 1:26). He saves those who are His worst enemies, like "Saul, yet breathing out threatenings and slaughter against the disciples of the Lord" (Acts 9:1). He turns men around who were content on the road to destruction. So good is He that He overcame our rebellion,

turning us in spite of ourselves, triumphing over our resistance when He could easily have left us alone.

6. God's goodness in providence is evident in *answering prayers*. The efficacy of prayer depends not on the manner of our petitions or the temper of our soul but on the goodness of the One to whom we pray. "If ye then, being evil, know how to give good gifts unto your children, how much more shall your Father which is in heaven give good things to them that ask him?" (Matt. 7:11). He loves the opportunity to show His goodness above that of earthly fathers. He would rather we ask for the greatest things heaven can afford than the trifles of this world. He is more liberal in giving than we are in desiring. How often He gives us more than we had the wisdom or confidence to ask!

7. God's goodness in providence is evident in *bearing with the infirmities of His people and accepting our imperfect obedience*. He beheld no iniquity in Jacob (Num. 23:21). How many kings of Judah were said to do right in God's sight, even though we read of sins they committed! God's omniscience knows their sins, but His goodness accepts their persons, in Christ.

8. God's goodness in providence is evident in *persecutions and afflictions*. "It is good for me that I have been afflicted; that I might learn thy statutes" (Ps. 119:71). In goodness, God removes from us, by means of afflictions, our false supports for security, our dross mixed in with gold, and that which would hinder our true happiness and usefulness. It is an act of kindness to prevent a man from falling down a cliff, though it be with a violent blow that lays him flat upon the ground. Hereby God sharpens our faith, moves us to pray, reveals ourselves and Himself like never before. So good is He that He goes with His people in their worst affliction. To Jacob He said, "I will go down with thee into Egypt; and I will also surely bring thee up again" (Gen. 46:4).

9. God's goodness in providence is evident in *temptations*. He is at the beginning and end of each one. God "will not suffer you

to be tempted above that ye are able; but will with the temptation also make a way to escape" (1 Cor. 10:13). He shortens the duration of temptations. The more severe, the less time God allots them. Christ's violent sufferings are repeatedly referred to in Scripture as an *hour*. He grants us strength to bear temptations in our time of need. He provides us with armor to resist the fiery darts and overcome the enemy of our souls. He gives great comforts during and after temptations. Job enjoyed a deeper knowledge of God and evidence of His love after the assaults against him than he ever had before. Though Peter was weak under temptation, the Lord sent him a special word through the angel: "Tell his disciples and Peter" (Mark 16:7). By means of temptations, God advances His grace in us. What a joy it is to prove God's goodness, and discover, by resisting temptation, that we had more grace than we had thought! God's goodness makes the devil a polisher while he intends to be a destroyer. Paul's thorn prevented his pride. Finally, God in goodness makes us more fit for service through the temptations we face. He tempers us in the furnace to make us better materials for His work. Peter was more fitted to strengthen the brethren, having been strengthened after his own failure.

May our good God now enable us to learn from this attribute and apply it to ourselves.

Instruction

1. It is a great sin to abuse God's goodness or hold it in contempt. This sin is common to all and is committed frequently. Every sin is ultimately a denial of the goodness of God, as if He had commanded that which was not in our best interest. Man's pursuit of sin shows that he perceives righteousness is bad for him and sin is good. All sins offend God, but sins against His goodness are especially heinous. "Despisest thou the riches of his goodness and forbearance and longsuffering; not knowing that the goodness of God leadeth thee to repentance? But after thy hardness and impenitent heart

treasurest up unto thyself wrath against the day of wrath and revelation of the righteous judgment of God" (Rom. 2:4–5). Sins against God's goodness call for His greatest indignation. "If ye forsake the LORD, and serve strange gods, then he will turn and do you hurt, and consume you, after that he hath done you good" (Josh. 24:20). Jerusalem, once His darling city, was turned into a field of blood because of its contempt against the goodness of God in Christ.

Now let us consider some ways in which men show their contempt for God's goodness:

- ❖ *By forgetting His benefits.* How quickly did Adam do exactly this! How quickly do we! The fact that the benefits are so bountiful and frequent ought to make us abound in thanksgiving, but instead we tend to despise them and forget how good God is to us.

- ❖ *By impatient murmuring.* In time of difficulty, man accuses God of cruelty, failing to see that all God's ways are good. After receiving so much goodness in the exodus, Israel murmured repeatedly against God. They foolishly spoke as if God had given them too much, and they wanted to return to the chains and taskmasters of Egypt. Man thinks himself to be better than God. Adam imagined that God was somehow envious of him, withholding good from him.

- ❖ *By unbelief and impenitence.* Why would men not come to God except that they doubt His goodness? The sending of the Son was the greatest act of goodness that God could express, and our refusing Him must be the highest reproach of that liberality.

- ❖ *By a distrust of His providence.* As trusting in Him supposes Him to be good, so distrusting supposes Him to be evil. First Peter 5:7 bids us cast all our cares upon Him, for

He cares for us. If we do not cast our cares on Him, it is a denial of His caring for us and of His goodness toward us.

❖ *By omissions of duty.* He who omits obedience to God is saying in effect, "I can do well without God; I do not need His goodness to sustain me."

❖ *By relying on our services to secure God's favor.* For example, in a time of great distress, a man makes an extraordinary vow to God that He might open up His goodness, as if God were withholding His goodness until He received a bribe.

❖ *By serving God only for His benefits rather than for Himself.* This reveals a sinful self-love: "lovers of pleasures more than lovers of God" (2 Tim. 3:4). It amounts to declaring that God is no better than us and that He is not the Supreme good.

❖ *By continuing in sin because of God's goodness*—that is, by employing the blessings of God in the gratifying of some lust or in the worship of some idol. Many who are blessed with wealth become boastful or wasteful. Many abuse God's gifts of earthly peace and security as opportunities to pursue sin with no danger of judgment. Many hoard their gain and clutch their luxury to their bosom, living only for self and despising the God who gave them what they have.

❖ *By ascribing our benefits to causes other than God's goodness.* We laud our own wisdom and effort, discarding God's goodness, as if He had nothing to do with our success. This again is idolatry.

2. If God is good, then man is certainly a fallen creature. The present state of mankind, full of sin and its effects, proves that a curse is in effect. God has revealed Himself as a judge, for man has violated His law.

3. There can be no just complaints against God for punishing those who abuse His goodness. God draws His sword only against those who have first slighted Him and His goodness. Who can blame God for vindicating His goodness upon the ungrateful despisers of it? God cannot be charged with injustice: He gave Adam the means to resist sin, and afterward gave the means to recover from it, yet all this is despised by us. God's goodness therefore warrants every stone laid in the foundation of hell.

4. God's goodness renders Him fit to govern the world. He is incapable of anything unworthy of His good nature. He cannot destroy any moral goodness in His creatures. Man's misery is all from himself. "O Israel, thou hast destroyed thyself" (Hos. 13:9). Not only is God fit to govern, but He also actually exercises His goodness in governing. It is unthinkable that divine goodness should create the world, and then abandon it in indifference. The continuing existence of the world today is a testimony to the goodness of God.

5. The goodness of God is the ground of all true religion and worship. It is the luster of all His attributes. All acts of devotion spring from God's liberality, either present or promised. His bounty allures us to Him. Job's wife tempted him by questioning God's goodness: "Curse God and die." But Job strengthened himself with this truth: "Shall we receive good at the hand of God, and shall we not receive evil?" (Job 2:9–10). That is, the goodness Job had enjoyed encouraged him to worship more than the evil he had suffered discouraged him from worship.

6. God's goodness renders Him beautiful and lovely. "For how great is his goodness, and how great is his beauty!" (Zech. 9:17). He is amiable to Himself. Only with Him is self-love proper, for there is none better than He who can lay claim to His affections. For this same reason, He ought to be amiable to us; there is none so good as He. If our affections find no attraction in Him, we are on the same low plane as devils. His sentiments of kindness especially make Him altogether lovely, more than any other attribute. Therefore, we are

under a strong obligation, not only because of His absolute goodness, which is the excellence of His nature, but also because of His relative goodness, which is goodness in operation toward us. His benefits to us are exceeding many and great, in creation, providence, and redemption. We in no way merit His goodness; rather, we are full of demerit. If we appreciate imperfect goodness in creatures, how much more ought we to prize perfect, infinite goodness in God? The whole reason why He ever manifested His goodness is so that He might be the object of our love, so that He might have a return of affection. There is nothing worthy of love besides Him.

7. God's goodness renders Him a fit object of our trust and confidence. His goodness is the ground of all our reliance upon Him. The psalmist ties these two ideas together, saying, "O taste and see that the Lord is good: blessed is the man that trusteth in him" (Ps. 34:8). Who is better than God? And who, then, is to be more trusted than God? His goodness is the first motive of our trust. If we see Him only as a judge, we will flee from Him. It is the goodness of God that draws us to Him and leads us to repentance (Rom. 2:4). Though His power is the foundation of trust, His goodness is the motive of trust. Under the law, the power of God was especially prominent; under the gospel, His goodness is more prominent. Thus, Hosea prophesied, "Afterward shall the children of Israel return, and seek the Lord their God, and David their king; and shall fear the Lord and his goodness in the latter days" (Hos. 3:5). Our trust in Him is glorifying to Him. We never please Him more than when we trust Him. He will never disappoint that faith that casts itself into the arms of His kindness.

8. God's goodness renders God worthy of our obedience and honor. An acquaintance with God's goodness should drive us to joyfully obey Him. "Thou art good, and doest good; teach me thy statutes" (Ps. 119:68). The riches of God's benefits toward us demand our submission to His will. We are debtors under the greatest of obligations because of the great advantages we enjoy by Him.

Even more, what renders our obedience a delight is knowing that all His demands are good. "His commandments are not grievous" (1 John 5:3). They are all for our good. A good God cannot require us to do evil.

Comfort

God in goodness is willing to forgive all who come to Him seeking mercy. "For thou, Lord, art good, and ready to forgive; and plenteous in mercy unto all them that call upon thee" (Ps. 86:5). He is patient to the failures of His children. If we offer the least thing sincerely, He will graciously receive it.

God's goodness comforts us in our prayers. Goodness delights to communicate itself. God is never weary of showing goodness; He delights to be petitioned. Therefore, we can pray with confidence and boldness, knowing that He welcomes our request. He has even given us a Mediator by whom to approach His throne. His goodness gives us every encouragement to draw near to Him.

God's goodness comforts us in our afflictions. Why should we fear when infinite goodness is for us? He always makes our afflictions to be consolations. "The LORD will give grace and glory: no good thing will he withhold from them that walk uprightly" (Ps. 84:11). Like Elijah, we dread to die at the hand of Jezebel, but we long to die at God's hand (1 Kings 19:2–4).

God's goodness assures us of happiness. It is the very nature of goodness to communicate itself. God would be deceiving us and working against Himself if He were not to satisfy the longings of His people and grant us Himself. His goodness first gave us these desires, and His goodness will fulfill them to the fullest extent of which our nature is capable, throughout all eternity.

God's goodness comforts us in time of danger. "The LORD is good, a strong hold in the day of trouble" (Nah. 1:7).

Exhortation

Let us earnestly desire God. Nothing else is worthy of our ardent thirst. It is utterly irrational not to desire Him. Man's will can only seek that which he perceives as good. Thus, Satan must disguise sin as good. But in God is true pure goodness, worthy of our deepest desire. Let us not be satisfied with trace amounts of derived goodness in creatures, but hunger after the fountainhead. All other sources are vain, but nothing in God will disappoint us. Rachel cried to Jacob, "Give me children, or else I die" (Gen. 30:1), and her last child cost her life. But if we cry, "Give me God, or else I die," our desire will be granted without any backfiring.

Let us often meditate on this attribute. In what better activity could we occupy our minds? Herein we are most elevated above brute beasts: we reflect upon the goodness of the hand that feeds us; we know the Author of our blessings. "The earth is full of the goodness of the LORD" (Ps. 33:5). Moreover, how many sins has He pardoned! How many chains has He broken! He Himself does what He loves in others: "God loveth a cheerful giver" (2 Cor. 9:7).

Meditating on this attribute will accomplish several things:

❖ *It will make us truly worship God.* "I will worship toward thy holy temple, and praise thy name for thy lovingkindness and for thy truth" (Ps. 138:2). Nothing motivates us to worship like a sense of God's goodness.

❖ *It will keep us humble.* Knowing that we have sinned against such a good God, there is no room for pride. Yet how gracious is He to us! How could anyone be proud of a gift he knows he does not deserve?

❖ *It will make us faithful to God.* How dare we waste our life on lesser things than our great Benefactor! Recipients of God's goodness are ennobled to live for the highest end.

❖ *It will make us patient under trials.* We trust Him to keep His golden promise of Romans 8:28, even though we cannot see how He will bring it to pass. He may give us a cloud, but never total darkness.

❖ *It will make us rise above the world.* A right comprehension of divine goodness will dull our appetite for worldly things and sharpen our desire for God Himself.

❖ *It will keep us from envy.* We will rejoice when God does good to someone else. "Is thine eye evil, because I am good?" (Matt. 20:15). For all we know, God is extending goodness to them so as to lead them to repentance (Rom. 2:4).

❖ *It will make us truly thankful.* Without deep thoughts of God's goodness, our praise descends into cold, formal rituals. This brings us to our next exhortation.

Let us be thankful for this attribute. "Bless the Lord, O my soul, and forget not all his benefits" (Ps. 103:2). God deserves constant praise for contriving our recovery, when we had plotted our ruin. Psalm 148 calls on inanimate creation to praise God: sun and moon, heavens and waters, fire, snow, wind, mountains, trees. How much more ought redeemed men worship with thankful hearts! Let us not misplace our praise upon some instrument that God has made use of!

Finally, let us imitate this attribute of God. "Do good to them that hate you . . . that ye may be the children of your Father which is in heaven" (Matt. 5:44–45). As God would not be perfect without goodness, so no Christian is perfect without kindness and charity. Scripture emphasizes two duties in this connection. First, we are to relieve and assist those in need. Is any too far beneath God to be an object of His care? Nor should any be beneath our concern. If God provides for beasts, ought we not to help our fellow man? Let us be stewards of God's gifts, not embezzlers. Let us learn that it is indeed "better to give than to receive" (Acts 20:35). God so delights in our imitating Him in this, that He promises to bless even a cup of cold water given for His glory (Matt. 10:42). Second, we are to be kind to our worst enemies. How kind God is to those who blaspheme His name with the breath He gives them! It is never a symptom of weakness or disgrace to resemble God. If His heart is open to us, let us not shut ours to any.

13

THE DOMINION OF GOD

Psalm 103:19 declares, "The LORD hath prepared his throne in the heavens; and his kingdom ruleth over all." This verse informs us that God is a king and that His kingdom extends everywhere. The term *Lord*, so frequently used in Scripture, plainly speaks of God's sovereign authority. David prayed, "Thine is the kingdom, O LORD, and thou art exalted as head above all" (1 Chron. 29:11–12). He is the "only Potentate, the King of kings" (1 Tim. 6:15).

God's dominion is threefold:

1. *His natural dominion.* He is absolutely sovereign over all things because He is their Creator.

2. *His gracious dominion.* He is sovereign over His redeemed ones in the covenant of grace.

3. *His glorious dominion.* As Judge, He will at last reign over all either in mercy or in justice.

General Propositions Concerning God's Dominion

We must distinguish between God's power or omnipotence and His authority. Power is His ability to do whatsoever He wills. Authority is His right to do the same. His authority or dominion is His moral power. A person may have great strength and yet have little or no authority. God has both. He has a right to command as well as a right to make all His commands obeyed or to punish those who violate His command. God's dominion is His right to make what

He pleases, possess what He has made, and dispose of what He possesses according to His pleasure.

This attribute is consistent with all the perfections of God. His goodness and wisdom render Him fit to rule. Without this attribute, justice and mercy would remain hidden in obscurity.

This attribute is universally acknowledged by every man's conscience. The law is written in our hearts (Rom. 2:15); therefore, there must be a lawgiver, a ruler, a governor. A man might as well deny the fact of his human nature as to deny God His nature.

The concept of sovereignty is essential to the whole concept of God. The fact that *God is* is inseparably connected with the fact that He is a rewarder of those who diligently seek Him (Heb. 11:6). As rewarder, He must be sovereign. Since God is the Creator, it is folly to deny full dominion to Him. Like the other attributes, His dominion is His essence; He cannot part with it, and it cannot exist apart from Him. No creature possesses this attribute. We cannot impose and enforce laws on the consciences of others. This prerogative is God's alone.

Wherein God's Dominion Is Founded

God's dominion is founded on the excellence of His nature. The more excellent the nature, the more fit to govern. God's superior intellect and moral perfection capacitate Him for dominion in a unique way. "I am God, and there is none like me. . . . I will do all my pleasure" (Isa. 46:9–10).

God's dominion is founded on His act of creation. He who gives being to a thing is the unquestionable owner of it. Since all things that exist were made by God, He is Lord over them all. When God defended His sovereignty to Job, His chief arguments were drawn from creation (see Job 38). The apostle Paul made the same point while preaching in Athens: "God that made the world and all things therein, seeing that he is Lord of heaven and earth" (Acts 17:24). When a man makes a thing, no one challenges his right to do whatever he pleases with it. Why should anyone even think of challenging God's absolute right over all He has created?

God's dominion is founded on the fact that He is the final end of all things. "The LORD hath made all things for himself" (Prov. 16:4). "For thy pleasure they are and were created" (Rev. 4:11). As the final end, God exercises sovereignty over the agents involved in any action.

God's dominion is founded on His preserving of all things. The ongoing dependence of all things on God argues for His dominion over them all.

God's dominion is strengthened by the benefits He bestows on His creatures. We are under a great obligation to Him because of the innumerable blessings of His goodness toward us. The inestimable blessing of redemption obligates us to serve Him. "Ye are not your own[.] For ye are bought with a price: therefore glorify God in your body, and in your spirit, which are God's" (1 Cor. 6:19–20). We usually say that the more a person pays for something, the more he deserves to have it. The high price God paid for our souls gives Him a special claim upon us.

The Nature of God's Dominion

God's dominion is independent. Among men, there must be the consent of the governed (except in parental authority). But God needs no permission to be God. He is not God because man voted to make Him so. There is no rule above Him because nothing is superior to Him.

God's dominion is absolute. His authority is unlimited. Properly speaking, the term *Lord* applies only to Him. All lesser lords are subject to Him who is Lord of lords.

God is free in His dominion over all things. He was totally free in creation to do whatever He desired. Preservation is also the fruit of His sovereignty—He could have annihilated earth after Adam's fall. Likewise, redemption is a sovereign act. God was under no more obligation to save fallen man than to save fallen angels. God has the right to legislate and to set the terms for every action. He sovereignly afflicts. He did not have to give us what we have, and He may remove what we have at His will. He is free to dispense His blessings unequally and to whom He chooses. He is free to inflict torments as He sees fit. God's right over His creatures is like that of a potter over his vessels. "Hath not the potter power over the clay, of the same lump to make one vessel unto honour, and another unto dishonour?" (Rom. 9:21). In fact, we might say that God has even more rights than the potter. The only difference between the potter and the vessel is that the potter has life, for both are made of clay! God sovereignly inflicts sickness. The disciples asked, "Master, who did sin, this man, or his parents, that he was born blind? Jesus answered, Neither hath this man sinned, nor his parents: but that the works of God should be made manifest in him" (John 9:2–3).

God is free in regard to any law outside Himself. Earthly kings are subject to laws in some form. But the King of all heaven and earth is under no law except Himself. He is rightly a law unto Himself.

God is free in that He is beyond the control of anyone. He has no superior to whom to give an answer. Certainly, we His creatures have no right to disagree with Him, as if we were greater than He. "None can stay his hand, or say unto him, What doest thou?" (Dan. 4:35). "O man, who art thou that repliest against God?" (Rom. 9:20).

God is free in regard to irresistibility. He possesses both might and right over all. He says, "I will work, and who shall let it?" (Isa. 43:13). No hand or multitude of hands can stop His hand. His decrees are certain.

Although God's dominion is absolute, it is not tyrannical. He does not act recklessly, arbitrarily, or capriciously. His sovereignty does not act independently of His other perfections. Rather, it is managed by wisdom, righteousness, and goodness. What appears to us as a purely sovereign act may have a depth of wisdom beneath it that we cannot see. It is impossible that God should act in an unfair or foolish manner for "the LORD is righteous in all his ways, and holy in all his works" (Ps. 145:17). His sovereignty does not deny His righteousness. Also, His sovereignty is inseparable from His goodness. Inasmuch as not punishing the sinner would be a denial of His justice, so tormenting an innocent person would be a denial of His goodness. His kingly throne is also a throne of grace (Heb. 4:16). He does not require servile obedience springing from fear but cheerful obedience springing from a sense of His goodness.

God's dominion extends over all creatures. The spacious firmament does not limit His authority. Everything He looks upon is under His rule. Heaven and its angels are under His authority. Thus, He is called *the Lord of hosts* hundreds of times in Scripture. "Bless ye the LORD, all ye his hosts; ye ministers of his, that do his pleasure" (Ps. 103:21). The sun must stand still at His command (Josh. 10:12). Hell and its demons are under His authority. They have forfeited His goodness, but they cannot escape His dominion. A prince is lord of his criminals as well as of his loyal subjects. God uses the natural malice of the devils for His own just purposes. "The deceived and the deceiver are his" (Job 12:16). Furthermore, earth and all its inhabitants are under God's authority. Locusts move at His command. Fire cannot consume without His leave. The waves rise and fall at His command. God's sovereignty extends over mankind. He determines the boundaries of nations (Acts 17:26). He especially rules over the hearts of men. Hebrews 12:9 calls Him "the Father of spirits." In granting a faculty of will to man, God has not divested Himself of His attribute of sovereignty. Man may rule the body of another, but not the soul. God only can work immediately in the soul to infuse habits that enable it to act nobly. Without any aid, God can change the will of man or give him a new heart. "The king's heart is in the hand of the LORD, as the rivers of water: he turneth it whithersoever he will" (Prov. 21:1). God can unlock the conscience and bring comfort or terror as He pleases. He can elevate the spirit of a persecuted saint despite racks and flames, and He can bring the rack and flames into the soul of an outwardly prosperous sinner.

God's dominion is eternal. "The LORD sitteth King for ever" (Ps. 29:10). His "throne [is] from generation to generation" (Lam. 5:19). There has never been any interruption to His rule.

Wherein God's Dominion Exists and How It Is Manifested

God acts sovereignly as lawgiver. He exercises His right to make laws. "For the LORD is our judge, the LORD is our lawgiver, the LORD is our king" (Isa. 33:22). His law is called "the royal law" (James 2:8). A command implies an authority in the commander and an obligation on the commanded. Properly speaking, there can be only one person who is not subject to laws and who makes laws instead—that person is God. "There is one lawgiver, who is able to save and to destroy" (James 4:12). All other authority is derived from this ultimate Source: "By me kings reign, and princes decree justice" (Prov. 8:15). God's right to legislate is universal, unlike that of an earthly king whose dominion ends at the ocean or the border of another nation. God's law is written in the heart of every man (Rom. 2:15). The reason for some of God's laws seems to be purely His own will. Though His moral law is certainly based in His character and glory, there are other laws for which we see no such clear reason. For example, the command to Adam not to eat of one tree was not based on anything inferior in that tree. It was as good for food as any of the others, but God used it as a mark of His sovereignty and of man's submission. Furthermore, the very manner in which He gave the moral law manifests His dominion: it was written with His finger in stone and accompanied by angels. Also, God acts sovereignly in the obligation of His law, which reaches into the conscience of man. No other person can bind the conscience but God, and once bound, no man can unbind it.

As sovereign lawgiver, God can do away with His law as freely as He gave it. We are not speaking here of His moral law, the disposal of which would be to deny God's own holiness and righteousness. But other laws He may relax at will. For example, He reversed the laws of nature when He parted the Red Sea. He repealed the ceremonial laws, which He gave to Israel, when the One whom these laws foreshadowed had come. We may even speak of His nullifying the covenant of works and enacting a covenant of grace, without which none of Adam's race would be blessed. Since all souls belong to Him, He may take away a life when and how He pleases. Had Abraham killed Isaac on his own, it would have been murder, but God sovereignly appointed Abraham as an executioner, and therefore he did not hesitate to obey the command.

As sovereign lawgiver, God punishes lawbreakers according to His will. This is His right as judge. If He did not punish offenders, His making of laws would lose all significance. Sovereignty is not preserved without justice. "The LORD is known by the judgment which he executeth" (Ps. 9:16). When He seems to have lost His dominion, He recovers it with punishment. Thus, He punished fallen angels and Adam upon their sin. He demonstrates His dominion in the means He employs in temporal punishments, whether it be frogs, armies, or angels.

God acts sovereignly as owner of all things. He freely chose from eternity a number of people to be objects of His grace. "He hath chosen us in him before the foundation of the world" (Eph. 1:4). Why did He write some names in His book and not others? If we pursue this question as far as possible, the answer is this: because it was "according to the good pleasure of his will" (Eph. 1:5). To Moses God said, "I will have mercy on whom I will have mercy, and I will have compassion on whom I will have compassion" (Rom. 9:15). If the reason drawn from God's sovereignty does not satisfy our inquiry, no other reason can be found. The reason for God's choice is not found in any merit in the ones He chose, for all men came from the same lump of sinful clay in Adam. We were all the children of wrath—we only merited punishment. Nor was the reason for God's choice based on any works He foresaw we would do. The only works foreseeable in sinners are corrupt works. He chose us "that we should be holy," not because we were already holy (Eph. 1:4). Our good works are the fruit, not the cause, of God's choice. He saves us so we might do good works and has determined those very works beforehand (Eph. 2:10). Even the faith by which we lay hold of Christ is given to us by God (Eph. 2:8). This gift is peculiar to the chosen ones: "according to the faith of God's elect" (Titus 1:1). If foreseen faith were the reason for God's choice, then God would be called our Elect, not we His elect. Men are not chosen because they believe; they believe because they are chosen. If anything foreseen were the reason for God's choice, He ought to have chosen angels since He could have foreseen much better service from them than from men. But He passed by fallen angels entirely and passed by some men as well. So free to act was He that He could have saved all or He could have saved none at all. Those who argue against God's liberty to choose must have a low view of sin and of God's character. They grant Him less sovereignty than an artisan has over his wood or stone. We should not think that God's choice was whimsical but rather that it was founded in wisdom beyond our capacity to grasp. In the end, the reason for God's choice is in Himself.

As owner of all, God bestows grace where He pleases. Though He is essentially good, He is not required to manifest all the treasures of His goodness to every person. If He were obligated to show goodness, no thanks would be due to Him. Who thanks the sun for shining on him when it can do nothing but shine? Again, He could have bestowed salvation on all men, but it was not His good pleasure to do so. It was not due to any lack of power in Him. Is unbelief greater than He? Does not the Spirit blow where He wishes (John 3:8)? Nor was His withholding grace due to any lack of goodness on the part of some. After all, He opens the minds of the most ignorant, converts the most sinful, and reaches down to the dregs of society. God owes no more of a debt to fallen man than to fallen angels. The bestowing of grace is simply an act of absolute sovereignty. As Pharaoh was free to honor the butler and execute the baker, God is free to save Abel but not Cain, Isaac but not Ishmael, Jacob but not Esau. Suppose a king proclaims pardon to a company of rebels, upon the condition they pay a sum of money, but they have lost their money and are reduced to a penniless state. Then suppose the king, out of pure generosity, sends some of them the money he requires of them, enabling them to meet the condition He set. His declaration of pardon was an act of sovereign authority; His providing the condition was an act of sovereign goodness. So it is with God and sinners.

As owner of all, God dispenses the means of grace to some but not all. He sends special revelation to some places but not to every place. He quickly removes it from some places while allowing others to enjoy a long benefit. Only Seth's line enjoyed special revelation until the flood. After the dispersing of the nations, only one family and nation enjoyed the means of grace—namely, Abraham and the nation that sprang from him. All the other nations were left in total or nearly total darkness. After Christ, that same nation descended into obscurity as to the gospel, while light dawned on the Gentiles. Why should Chorazin and Bethsaida enjoy the benefits that were not granted to Tyre and Sidon, except for divine appointment? Why should America have been left in such darkness for so long and now enjoy such light, except for sovereign determination? "Even so, Father: for so it seemed good in thy sight" (Matt. 11:26).

As owner of all, God determines the influence of the means of grace. Not all who hear the gospel are converted. Some who hear are spiritualized, but others are merely moralized. Sometimes the gospel conquers thousands; other times, barely tens. Sometimes the harvest is great where the laborers are but few, and sometimes the harvest is small where the laborers are many. Remember, it is the same gospel! What then is the reason for such variety, save that God would increase the proofs of His own sovereignty? Therefore, let us have adoring thoughts of the sovereignty of God and not murmur against it. Let us humbly thank Him for what we have received and humbly ask Him for what we need. To own God as a sovereign in a way of dependence is the way to be owned by Him as subjects in a way of favor.

As owner of all, God gives a greater measure of knowledge to some than others. "He giveth wisdom unto the wise, and knowledge to them that know understanding" (Dan. 2:21). He gifted Bezaleel "in wisdom, and in understanding, and in knowledge, and in all manner of workmanship" (Ex. 31:3). Paul had a clearer understanding than Peter concerning the abolition of the ceremonial law (Galatians 2). The Holy Spirit works "dividing to every man severally as he will" (1 Cor. 12:11).

As owner of all, God calls some to special service in their generation. Though Moses was a great man, Aaron was appointed as high priest. David's older brothers were passed by when Samuel anointed him. God prepares and equips some vessels for a more public ministry and others for a more obscure one.

As owner of all, God bestows honor and wealth as He pleases. The Lord is the maker of both rich and poor (Prov. 22:2). One has a crown over his head; another has scarcely a roof over his head. A scepter is placed in one man's hand, and a spade in another's. Joseph was free to bless Benjamin with more changes of clothes than the other brothers. God wrongs no man if He lets him languish out his days in poverty and disgrace. According to Psalm 55:19, we are subject to the changes appointed to us by God in this life so that we might fear Him.

As owner of all, God dispenses His gifts when He wills. As He is the Lord of His own grace, so He is the Lord of the times and seasons when to display it.

God acts sovereignly as governor. He disposes of states and kingdoms. Daniel said, "He changeth the times and the seasons: he removeth kings" (2:21). God caused an anonymous, haphazard arrow to find the chink in Ahab's armor. And though Ahab had seventy sons, none of them lived to succeed him on the throne. God said concerning another king, "Now have I given all these lands into the hand of Nebuchadnezzar the king of Babylon, my servant; and the beasts of the field have I given him also to serve him" (Jer. 27:6). Man tends to confine his thoughts to second causes and fails to see God's hand behind those causes. God is as much in control of the throne in the palace as of the stool in the cottage.

As governor, God raises up and orders the spirits of men. Man's will is a finite principle and is subject to Him who possesses infinite sovereignty over all things. Moses was rescued by the daughter of the very king who had vowed to destroy him. God even caused him to be educated in the king's own house. Cyrus did not know God was at work in him when he decreed the rebuilding of the Jews' temple (Isa. 45:4).

As governor, God restrains the passions of men. Sometimes He does this outwardly, as at the Tower of Babel, but usually He does this by an inward curbing of passions when there is no visible cause. Thus, He kept the Canaanites from desiring Israel's land when they were at Jerusalem celebrating their annual feasts (Ex. 34:24). Laban pursued Jacob intending to do him harm, but God said to him in a dream, "Take heed that thou speak not to Jacob either good or bad" (Gen. 31:24).

As governor, God defeats the plans and efforts of men. He is seen as laughing at man's best purposes, schemes, and devices (Ps. 2:4). He is privy to all secret counsels of men. "O Lord, I know that the way of man is not in himself: it is not in man that walketh to direct his steps" (Jer. 10:23). He makes a Haman to be hanged on the gallows he constructed for Mordecai, while Mordecai is exalted instead. The Jews thought crucifying Christ would keep the Romans from coming (John 11:48), but instead, this deed hasted their destruction at the hands of the Roman armies.

As governor, God sends judgments upon whom He pleases. "I kill, and I make alive; I wound, and I heal" (Deut. 32:39). Not every Sodom is destroyed by fire from heaven. Yet all armies of heaven and earth are at His disposal and take their orders from Him to execute His vengeance.

As governor, God appoints every man his calling and status in this world. He numbers the hairs of our head. He appoints our work or occupation in this world, which is known as our *calling*.

As governor, God determines the means and occasions of the conversions of men. At first, Paul's imprisonment may have seemed a tragedy. But some of Caesar's servants would be converted by hearing the gospel from this prisoner. Some have gone to hear a preacher simply in order to mock but, being awakened by God, remained to pray. The same sermon that converts one may harden another.

As governor, God disposes of the lives of men. He holds the key to the womb and to death. David wrote, "My times are in thy hand" (Ps. 31:15). God appoints various lengths of life and various measures of health according to His sovereign will.

God acts sovereignly as redeemer. In the work of redemption, this dominion is exercised not only over man but also over Christ the Son. Thus, God is called the "head of Christ" (1 Cor. 11:3), not in terms of the divine essence, which is coequal with the Father, nor in terms of His human nature but in terms of the economy of redemption. The whole gospel is nothing but a declaration of God's sovereign pleasure concerning Christ and concerning us in Him.

God sovereignly required satisfaction for man's sin. Had He never required such a satisfaction, He would effectively have laid aside His authority altogether. But God sovereignly appointed Christ to the work of redemption. He was a Son by nature but a

Mediator by divine will. He is called an "Apostle" (Heb. 3:1)—that is, a messenger sent by God. He said to the Father, "I come . . . to do thy will, O God" (Heb. 10:7). As God was at liberty to create or not to create, so He was at liberty to redeem or not to redeem. It was an act of His sovereignty to transfer our sins upon Christ. Only the supreme ruler in a land can commute a sentence of punishment. Even so, God summed up our debts and charged them to Christ's account, holding Him responsible as our Surety. Had the Son simply taken upon Himself to incarnate and die, His death would have been simply physical and temporal. But God made Him who knew no sin to be sin for us (2 Cor. 5:21). God set Him forth and delivered Him up (Rom. 3:25; 8:32). Therefore, His death was effectual to redeem those in whose place He suffered. The imputation of our sin to Him and of His righteousness to us is an act of pure sovereignty. In the economy of redemption, God commanded Christ to be the Redeemer; it was a matter of obedience. Christ says, "Thy law is within my heart" (Ps. 40:7). Furthermore, God sovereignly exalted Christ after His death: God gave Him all authority (Matt. 28:18), gave Him to be head over all things to the church (Eph. 1:22), gave Him a name above every name (Phil. 2:9), and committed all judgment to Him (John 5:22). Thus, God is sovereign in all that Christ has done as a priest or shall do as a king.

Now let us apply to our hearts this wonderful attribute.

Instruction

God's sovereignty is held in great contempt by natural man. Man would rather be a slave to sin than to God. This is the great quarrel between God and man: Who shall be the ruler? If it were left up to man, God would not rule in even one village on the whole earth. Sinful man cannot endure even one authoritative law from God. "Ye have set at nought all my counsel" (Prov. 1:25). To slight God's sovereignty is to stab His deity for He cannot be God without His authority.

In general, all sin is a contempt of God's dominion. Every sin defies His law and, hence, the authority behind it. "The carnal mind . . . is not subject to the law of God" (Rom. 8:7). We set up our will above God's will. As Satan first desired to escape from God's dominion and be equal to God, so he tempted man with the same evil thought: "Ye shall be as gods" (Gen. 3:5). It is the universal language of man to disown God's dominion. "Let us break their bands asunder, and cast away their cords from us" (Ps. 2:3). Every man in his own way says, "I do not care what God has said; I am determined to live life my way." Even religious man usurps the authority of God. For example, the Church of Rome withholds the cup from the people in the Lord's Supper, which Christ commanded them to drink. Many such things they do, as if God had divested Himself of the title of King of Kings and transferred it to the bishop of Rome. Most of the errors of men may be summed up as a denial of God's sovereignty.

More specifically, men scorn this attribute by denying God His rights as lawgiver, owner, or governor. God is held in contempt as lawgiver when men make laws contrary to those He has established or when they seek to bind another's conscience or when they make additions to God's law. Though Peter dared not be a lord over God's heritage (1 Peter 5:3), those who claim to be his successors reign as lords, bringing in many innovations God did not ordain and some which He forbade. The Lawgiver is despised when men prefer to obey man's laws before God's. This is but to set man above God. When we outwardly obey one of God's commands because it is backed by human authority, we show a higher regard for man than for God.

God is held in contempt as owner of all when men envy. The foundation of this emotion is a disagreement with God concerning His distribution of His goods. Likewise with the sins of stealing and cheating: they are committed against God Himself. His ownership rights are also denied when we use what God has given us for our own selfish ends rather than for that which God has revealed. We must remember that we are stewards of God—our holdings belong to Him. Therefore, we must not covet nor needlessly waste nor withhold from the needy. We must not use religion as a means of honoring ourselves rather than God.

God is held in contempt as governor when men worship idols or adore any creature instead of God. No matter how great the idol, God alone is worthy of our love. A woman is an adulteress regardless of whether her lover be a prince or a pauper. God alone is worthy of our affection and trust. But we hold Him in contempt when we rely on anything more than we rely on Him. It is not unlawful to have wealth and honor, but when we love them and rely on them above Him, we deny Him His place of sovereignty in our souls. We must never prefer the authority of clay above that of heaven nor serve the servant instead of the King. Any time we are impatient or murmur under providence, we in effect wish that God were off His throne and that His crown were placed upon our own head. This is a dreadful copy of Adam's original sin. When men are proud and presuming and speak more like a god than a man, they disdain God's government. They say, "To day or to morrow we will go into such a city, and continue there a year, and buy and sell, and get gain." But they ought to acknowledge God's dominion and say, "If the Lord will, we shall live, and do this, or that" (James 4:13, 15). If we possess a self-willed, independent spirit and insist that no man have authority over us, we are rebelling against God's authority that He has delegated in earthly relationships. Slight and careless worship of God is another way of showing contempt against the Sovereign of the universe. Those who refuse to bow are little worse than those who bow halfway. God demanded the best of the flock for sacrifice, and we must bring Him our best and heartiest worship. Sins of omission show a contempt for our Governor, as if we were free to choose when to obey and when to leave off obedience. Finally, when we unjustly judge and censure others, we usurp God's rights, claiming a superiority over the law, as if men were more under our authority than under God's. "He that speaketh evil of his brother, and judgeth his brother, speaketh evil of the law, and judgeth the law: but if thou judge the law, thou art not a doer of the law, but a judge. There is one lawgiver, who is able to save and to destroy: who art thou that judgest another?" (James 4:11–12). Our brother is not to be governed by our whims but by God's law and his own conscience.

God not only has the right to govern the world but He actually exercises that right. Should such a glorious quality as this lie idle? Is God like some lazy monarch who ignores his kingdom and spends all his time in his gardens? It would be unrighteous for God not to use His dominion for righteous ends.

Since God is sovereign, He can do no wrong. He does nothing but that which He has a sovereign right to do. Even when He takes away our lives, He takes only that which He gave in the first place. He is no debtor to us. The owner of all things has every right to seize His goods in order to vindicate His honor. We were made by Him and for Him. "Of him, and through him, and to him, are all things: to whom be glory for ever. Amen" (Rom. 11:36).

Since God is sovereign, all merit from creatures is totally excluded. The very faculties by which we render obedience to Him are granted to us by Him. Does a servant earn merit with his lord because he uses the tools his lord provided him? Whatever we give to God is already His. The only way He can become indebted to us is if He freely obligates Himself by His own promise.

Since God is absolute sovereign, all those in authority on this earth are under His authority. Earthly lords are simply God's lieutenants, more at His disposal than their subjects are to them. Earthly powers are no more than a silly fly between the fingers of a giant. It follows, therefore, that those who rule should rule according to God's revealed will, setting an example of submission for their subjects to follow. They should imitate God's justice in all their administrations. And we should obey them when they act accordingly. How can we say we are friends to God when we are enemies of his lieutenants? Christ Himself was no enemy to Caesar.

Conviction

The consideration of the dominion of God ought to produce great fear and dread in all who rebel against it. This was the inlet to all other sins. The forbidden tree was not naturally inferior to any others in the garden, but it became the test for man's submission. Adam defiantly ate of it. God's question to him emphasizes His authority that was spurned: "Hast thou eaten of the tree, whereof I commanded thee that thou shouldest not eat?" (Gen. 3:11). God's dominion cannot be despised without meriting the greatest punishment. He not only has the right to vindicate Himself by inflicting such punishment but if He did not do so, He would appear to despise His dominion. The floating carcass of Pharaoh is a testimony to all who would dare challenge God's sovereignty and say, "Who is the LORD, that I should obey his voice?" (Ex. 5:2). Because of this despised attribute, punishment for sin is unavoidable. "With God is terrible majesty" (Job 37:22). Who can escape from God? Who can give comfort once God visits with judgment? There is no place of safety from this Sovereign. He can make any part of His creation an instrument of wrath. His hand holds unlimited weapons. He can turn every comfort against you. His punishment is terrible beyond compare and beyond description. What folly to despise such a mighty Sovereign!

Comfort

Thank God, there is also comfort to be derived from this attribute for those who bow to His scepter! All His other attributes would afford little relief without this one. His love to His people is as great as His sovereignty over them. If He pardons our sins, who can repeal or reverse it? With Him is full security. He will most certainly subdue the corruptions of His people. He assures our happiness by en-suring our holiness. He is bigger than the biggest sin that indwells us. This attribute affords every encouragement to pray to God. He has as much tenderness as authority and is pleased with prayer since it acknowledges His dominion. This attribute comforts us in our af-flictions for we know He appoints them for us. This exercise of His authority in sending us afflictions is coupled with the exercise of His goodness and wisdom. The tempest that tore our ship will drive us into our heavenly port. This attribute comforts us when God's cause in the earth seems defeated. His enemies cannot pull His hook out of their mouth. "There is no wisdom nor understanding nor counsel against the LORD" (Prov. 21:30). He can dismount Pharaoh's chariot wheels at His pleasure. The devil himself must be still when God issues him a sovereign order. How often has God turned the en-emies' swords into their own bowels! God cannot be anything but victorious.

Meditation

We should habitually think of our great King and acknowledge Him as our Lord and ourselves as His subjects. This acknowledgment was what God required of Cain and was the purpose for which He sent the plagues upon Egypt—"that ye may know how that I am the LORD" (Ex. 10:2).

> *Meditating on this attribute will make Him the object of our trust.* He alone will never disappoint us. This attribute should pry our hands off every other holding so that we might grasp Him. We must trust God only, regardless of the presence or absence of second causes.

> *Meditating on this attribute will make us diligent in worship.* When we come before Him, the whole demeanor of our souls and bodies should reflect the majesty and authority of the One we worship. "Keep thy foot when thou goest to the house of

God" (Eccl. 5:1). We should not hear God's Word as if it were the voice of some ordinary peasant.

Meditating on this attribute will make us charitable to others. Since God has prospered us, how can we not honor Him with our substance? We must make others the recipients of our benevolence. How eager was Paul to collect relief for the needy saints and to see it delivered to them!

Meditating on this attribute will make us watchful against temptations. If we can but remember God's dominion over us, we would soon beat back the temptation and send it into retreat.

Meditating on this attribute will make us endure afflictions rightly. We must view them as a check from heaven for our good. "Despise not thou the chastening of the Almighty" (Job 5:17).

Meditating on this attribute will make us resign ourselves to God in everything. We must never call God into account, as if we were His judges rather than His worms. Jonah did not do well to be angry. Eli spoke truth when he said, "It is the LORD: let him do what seemeth him good" (1 Sam. 3:18).

Meditating on this attribute will stop our vain curiosity. Our Lord answered Peter's desire to know of John's fate with these words, "If I will that he tarry till I come, what is that to thee? Follow thou me" (John 21:22). God has the right to reveal and to conceal. We are to fulfill our duty and lay aside curiosity.

Exhortation

From this attribute, let us learn humility. We are never abased until we have a sense of God's excellence and eminence. Job was never so abased as after a great display of God's sovereignty. Having recognized God as "the Judge of all the earth" (Gen. 18:25), Abraham confessed that he himself was "but dust and ashes" (v. 27). What madness for a creature to prance like a creator! There is more distance between God and man than between being and not being. There is no place for pride before God. How carelessly we speak of owning things! Is anything really ours? Is it not all—even our very lives—lent to us from God?

Let us learn praise and thankfulness. "Sing praises unto our King, sing praises. For God is the King of all the earth: sing ye praises with understanding" (Ps. 47:6–7). He who has given us power to praise is Himself the subject of our praise. He might have dashed us against the wall, as a potter does a vessel. Had He done so, none would have the right to question His action. Our only question is one of amazement and worship: "What is man, that thou art mindful of him? and the son of man, that thou visitest him?" (Ps. 8:4). His goodness is sovereign. He is the fountain of all our supplies, and all praise be unto Him!

Let us promote the honor and glory of God. Again, Romans 11:36 supplies the reason: "For of him, and through him, and to him, are all things: to whom be glory for ever. Amen." All our thoughts and actions ought to be addressed to His glory. Our whole being ought to be consecrated to His honor. He that makes himself his own end makes himself his own sovereign. We think ourselves more than creatures if we are too good to deny ourselves for the sake of our sovereign Creator. God will call our stewardship into account. He is too gracious a Sovereign to neglect those who are mindful of His glory. He says, "Them that honor me I will honor" (1 Sam. 2:30).

Let us fear and revere God for who He is. Any other response is woefully inadequate. "Who would not fear thee, O King of nations?" (Jer. 10:7). The dominion of God, considered with the goodness of His dominion, is one of the first sparks that ignites the fire of true religion.

Let us pray to and trust in God. The model prayer concludes, "Thine is the kingdom" (Matt. 6:13). If God is not sovereign, we ought not to waste time praying to Him nor trusting in Him. Instead, we ought to rely on our own dominion and ingenuity. Such a thought is blasphemous.

Let us obey God. This is perhaps the most obvious deduction from this attribute. As justice requires fear, goodness requires thankfulness, faithfulness requires trust, truthfulness requires belief, even so sovereignty requires obedience. If sovereignty is the first notion a creature has concerning God, surely obedience ought to be the first motion in us. Anything less is a contradiction of what we know and profess. "Why call ye me, Lord, Lord, and do not the things which I say?" (Luke 6:46).

Why should we obey God?

❖ *Because obedience is the only proper response to Him.* The whole arrangement of things makes this only reasonable.

❖ *Because it is honorable and advantageous to us.* Serving Him is a high honor. Better to bow before a heavenly throne than to sit on an earthly one. Also, it is a part of God's sovereignty and greatness to reward any service done for Him.

❖ *Because God sovereignly requires obedience from man.* No sooner had He placed Adam in the garden than He gave him commands to obey. "And the LORD God took the man, and put him into the garden of Eden to dress it and to keep it. And the LORD God commanded the man, saying, Of every tree of the garden thou mayest freely eat: But of the tree of the knowledge of good and evil, thou shalt not eat of it" (Gen. 2:15–17). God prefaced the Ten Commandments with a statement of His sovereignty: "I am the LORD thy God, which have brought thee out of the land of Egypt, out of the house of bondage. Thou shalt have no other gods before me" (Ex. 20:2–3).

❖ *Because all lesser creation obeys Him.* The sea stays in its bounds. The stars march in their order. Lions in the den obey Him. And should not the creature made in God's likeness obey? Let us not pretend to obey while acting as rebels.

How should we obey God?

❖ *With a respect for His authority.* If a man refrains from drunkenness simply because it is bad for his health, he has set up himself, not God, as the authority. True obedience has a view to the authority that gave the command.

❖ *With our best and most exact obedience.* His greatness deserves and demands it. The more noble a man is, the more careful we are in our manner of service to him.

❖ *With sincere, inward obedience.* Unlike man's laws, God's laws reach into our very hearts. Therefore, our obedience is incomplete if it is void of a sincere heart.

❖ *With obedience that is unto God alone.* "Thou shalt worship the Lord thy God, and him only shalt thou serve" (Matt. 4:10). The obedience we render to man is with a view toward God ultimately. Servants are to be obedient unto their masters "as unto Christ . . . doing the will of God from the heart" (Eph. 6:5–6).

❖ *With obedience that is all-encompassing.* Some laws of men are not to be obeyed (Acts 4:19; 5:29). But all God's laws are righteous, and therefore, all are to be obeyed. We have no right to pick and choose which of His commands we will respect.

❖ *With an indisputable obedience.* We must render prompt and ready obedience, like Abraham who did not hesitate or balk at God's command to offer up Isaac. God has an indisputable right to command, and we have an indisputable duty to obey Him.

❖ *With joyful obedience.* Begrudging service is a discredit to a master. The quality of the master renders the service more enjoyable. And who is a master so great as God? Let us show the world we serve a good Master. We should obey Him not because we must but because we will. Involuntary obedience is not worthy of the name.

❖ *With a perpetual obedience.* As long as God is God, and as long as man is a creature, we owe Him our obedience.

Let us be patient. It is not becoming for the clay to lose patience with the potter. It is our part to gladly submit to His sovereign will in all things. Though Job's patience was imperfect at first, he is presented as an example to us. "Ye have heard of the patience of Job" (James 5:11). After his trials, he was exceeding patient, willing to stand in utter silence and submission before his Sovereign (Job 40:4; 42:2). If we have a right to smite our beasts for our good when we please simply because we are their owners, how much more right does God have to smite us for our good, seeing He owns us? How foolish it is to not submit patiently to God! Since we cannot subdue Him, it is better for us to submit to Him.

The very nature and essence of patience is submission to God's sovereignty. Job exemplified this when he said, "The LORD gave, and the LORD hath taken away; blessed be the name of the LORD" (1:21). To be patient because we cannot avoid it is not a loyal patience. Such is the patience of a prisoner who longs to escape. But to submit because God has done it is the true grace. "Though he slay me, yet will I trust in him" (Job 13:15). The sovereign greatness of God claims an undivided respect from His creatures.

14

THE PATIENCE OF GOD

Nahum prophesied against Nineveh. Though in man's sight God's judgment on the Assyrian capital was slow in coming, it would undoubtedly come. Only the patience of God withheld it. "The LORD is slow to anger, and great in power, and will not at all acquit the wicked: the LORD hath his way in the whirlwind and in the storm, and the clouds are the dust of his feet" (Nah. 1:3). Notice the connection between God's power and His patience. His power over Himself is the cause of His slowness to wrath. When Moses interceded for Israel in Numbers 14:17, he asked God to be patient, praying, "I beseech thee, let the power of my lord be great." God has power over Himself to sustain great injuries without an immediate revenge. He has a power of patience as well as a power of justice.

We should not think of God's patience as if He were suffering, as is often true of man's patience. Rather, God's patience is a willingness to defer His wrath upon sinful creatures. No matter how much a person suffers in this life, he suffers less than he deserves, thanks to the patience of God. Other parallel terms in Scripture include *longsuffering, forbearance,* and *keeping silence.* This attribute is one that God Himself proclaimed to Moses saying, "The LORD, The LORD God, merciful and gracious, longsuffering" (Ex. 34:6).

The Nature of God's Patience

In some respects, God's patience is distinct from His goodness and mercy. Mercy views the creature as miserable; patience views him as criminal. Mercy pities the sinner himself; patience bears with his sin. Mercy would have no room to act if patience did not prepare the way; patience is the first whisper of mercy. Goodness extends to all creatures in their original state and to all earthly creatures in their lapsed state; patience regards man in particular, considered as a guilty creature. The deferment of punishment for fallen angels cannot properly be called patience, for where there is no proposal of mercy, there is no exercise of patience. Patience is a temporary sparing to allow a change of heart. Had sin not entered, God would never have exercised patience.

God's patience is not grounded upon any weakness in Himself. It is not that He is incapable of anger or ignorant of provocations or slack concerning His promise. He sees and considers every sin and will "set them in order before thine eyes" (Ps. 50:21).

God's patience is not constrained by cowardice, feebleness of spirit, or want of strength, as is often the case with men. God's power has not diminished since He created the world out of nothing. But one word from His lips would send all creation into the nothingness from which it came. Or He could take away the life of any person at any moment.

Rather than a lack of power over creatures, the ground of God's patience is a fullness of power over Himself. The weaker a person is, the less control he has over his passions. Therefore, the proverb says, "He that is slow to anger is better than the mighty; and he that ruleth his spirit than he that taketh a city" (16:32). But God has such a command over Himself that He is without passions like men. His exercise of patience is a greater argument for His power than His creating the universe. He endures with much longsuffering the vessels of wrath to make His power known (Rom. 9:22). We see more of His power in His patience than in His wrath.

The exercise of God's patience is founded in the death of Christ. This is evident because God shows no patience toward the fallen angels; He bound them over for punishment as soon as they had sinned. Christ did not die for them. But He did die for men. Even those men whom He did not savingly redeem in His death receive certain temporal benefits from it; especially, they enjoy God's patience. In this sense, Christ is said to have "bought" those who "bring upon themselves swift destruction," and whose "damnation slumbereth not" (2 Peter 2:1, 3). He purchased the continuance of their life and the stay of their execution so that offers of grace might be made to them. As grace was not discovered except in Christ, so patience was not discovered except in Christ. The coming of Christ was the reason for God's patience in the Old Testament time. The gathering of His elect is the reason for His patience now.

No other attributes hinder God's exercise of patience. God's truthfulness in threatening punishment is not violated simply because He waits a long time to carry out the threat. In the forty-day notice given to Nineveh through Jonah, the implied message was that upon condition of their repentance, the city would be spared. Likewise, the threat to Adam of death upon eating the forbidden fruit was not carried out as far as eternal death is concerned because a Surety was found whose death more honored God than if Adam himself had died. Nor does God's patience disagree with His justice and righteousness. We never find fault with a judge who postpones a trial or sentencing or execution for a good reason. And let none think that God has no good reasons for His patience! He is not willing that any of His people should perish (2 Peter 3:9)—the longsuffering is *toward us*, that is, God's elect to whom the promise is made. God has glorified His justice on Christ, and His patience now is in perfect harmony with His justice. Moreover, God is free to choose the time that pleases Him best for the punishment of evildoers. The times and seasons are in the Father's own power (Acts 1:7). Justice has all eternity to demonstrate itself, but patience has time as its only opportunity. Instead of being violated, justice is made more visible by God's patience: every objection against justice will be more than removed because of the great patience God has shown to sinners.

How God's Patience Is Manifested

Consider some general instances on how God's patience is manifested:

❖ *He manifested His patience to Adam and Eve.* He could have struck them dead the moment they first considered the temptation in a positive light, for it was then that the sin began. Their eating was more the end of the act than its beginning. Instead, God allowed Adam to live for 930 years. His allowing the race to continue to this day is a testimony to His patience.

❖ *God manifested His patience to the Gentiles.* Their crimes described in Romans 1 are abundantly sufficient to bring down Almighty wrath in a moment. Yet God is so exceedingly patient that He "winked" at "the times of this ignorance" (Acts 17:30). He winked as if He did not see them. He did not call them presently into account for their sin.

❖ *God manifested His patience to Israel.* Though God knew them to be a stiff-necked people, He "suffered . . . their manners in the wilderness" (Acts 13:18). He bore with them for about fifteen hundred years, from the time of the Exodus to the destruction of the city of Jerusalem by the Romans.

Now let us consider some specific ways in which God manifests this attribute:

1. He gives advance warnings of coming judgments. Many pages of the Old Testament are full of these warnings. How many prophets God sent with messages of impending doom! Enoch and Noah

warned the antediluvians. Every remarkable judgment on Israel was foretold, from the famine in Egypt foretold by Joseph to the desolation of Jerusalem foretold by Christ. The evident purpose of the warnings was so that He might not pour out His wrath. Before He strikes, He lifts up His hand and shakes His rod so that men might see and avoid the stroke. Through Jonah, God threatened Nineveh with destruction so that its repentance might make void the prophecy. God roars like a lion that men might hear His voice and shelter themselves from being torn by His wrath.

2. God long delays His threatened judgments, even though the rebels do not repent. How often the "sentence against an evil work is not executed speedily" (Eccl. 8:11)! While He prepares His arrows, He is waiting for an occasion to lay them aside and dull their points. To Israel He said, "I have no pleasure in the death of him that dieth" (Ezek. 18:32). He patiently restrained His wrath upon Sodom until it would have wronged His justice to restrain it any longer. He bore with the iniquity of the Amorites four hundred years (Gen. 15:16). He prolonged Ahab's judgment upon a mere shadow of humiliation. He waited forty years to avenge Himself upon the generation that crucified His only begotten Son.

3. When He can delay no longer, God carries out His threats with some sense of unwillingness. "He doth not afflict willingly [literally, from His heart] nor grieve the children of men" (Lam. 3:33). Prophecies loaded with threats of judgment are called *the burden of the Lord* not only because they are a burden to those who receive them but also to the God who sends them. In the flood we see the same regret: "And it repented the LORD that he had made man on the earth, and it grieved him at his heart" (Gen. 6:6). Or consider His words in Hosea 6:4, "O Ephraim, what shall I do unto thee? O Judah, what shall I do unto thee?" Thus, the psalmist explains, "Many a time turned he his anger away, and did not stir up all his wrath" (78:38), as if He were indecisive as to what to do. Once the

judgment falls, it falls in degrees. First comes the palmerworm, then the locust, then the cankerworm, and then the caterpillar (Joel 1:4).

4. God moderates His judgments when He sends them. He does not empty His quiver of His arrows; He opens not all His store. Often He punishes just a few, making them examples, when He could have punished the whole lot. Ezra prayed, "Thou our God hast punished us less than our iniquities deserve" (9:13). God did not curse the earth that it should bring forth no fruit but that it should bring forth fruit only by the wearisome toil of man. In our punishments, God supports us.

5. God patiently continues to give great mercies after we have provoked Him. While man continues in sin, God continues in outward mercies. Israel murmured at the Red Sea, yet God wrought a monumental deliverance there.

6. All this is amazing when we consider our many provocations against God. Let us not underestimate the enormity of our sins. Every one of them is a high treason against the King of heaven. His justice, holiness, and omniscience all call out for judgment, but sheer patience arrests the judgment for a season. The number of our sins is staggering beyond calculation. How many sins does one man commit in a lifetime? How many sins of omission can be laid to his charge? How many provocations arise to heaven from the whole earth in just one day? And consider how long God has been patient with this world. For six thousand years, every corner of earth has partaken of the riches of His goodness, forbearance, and longsuffering. Not one sin has ever been hidden from Him; all are open to His view. How great is God's patience! The angels would be glad to have an order from the throne to destroy this wicked world at once—only God's patience stops their fury.

Why God Exercises So Much Patience

By exercising patience, God shows Himself appeasable. He shows Himself not implacable but reconcilable. His patience lets men know they would find God favorable to them if they did but seek after Him. The fact that He did not destroy Adam and Eve at once but bore with them demonstrated patience and gave man hope of something better to come, even though that *something* was yet to be clearly revealed. Even the heathen, who only witness God's glory in the heavens (Ps. 19:1), should deduce that the One who created is merciful, despite all their offenses against Him. In doing "good, and [giving] us rain from heaven, and fruitful seasons, filling our hearts with food and gladness" (Acts 14:17), God is not pretending to be a friend to His enemies but is showing Himself friendly indeed, giving them encouragement to repent and some ground to hope for pardon.

By exercising patience, God gives men ample opportunity to repent. He says exactly this concerning Jezebel in the church at Thyatira: "I gave her space to repent of her fornication" (Rev. 2:21). Peter wrote that "the longsuffering of our Lord is salvation" (2 Peter 3:15)—that is, God's patience is a solicitation to men to attend to the means of salvation. Peter goes on to say that Paul, by inspiration, had written the same thing, evidently referring to Romans 2:4, which says that God's goodness leads to repentance. God's goodness and longsuffering take us by the hand and point us where we should go. Since all men by nature know that sinners deserve God's judgment (Rom. 1:22), they cannot rationally misconstrue God's patience as an approval of their sin. Sound reasoning tells them that God's slowness to anger and His willingness to turn His arrows of judgment another way are unmistakable tokens of divine patience.

The exercise of God's patience allows for the propagation of mankind. Without patience, no race would have proceeded from Adam. God's honor would have been impaired, since "He created [the earth] not in vain, he formed it to be inhabited" (Isa. 45:18).

God exercises patience for the continuance of His covenant people. This is God's special purpose. He is patient with mankind in general, for out of it He calls His elect to salvation. They spring from the stock of sinners. A woman who is guilty of a capital crime is not executed if she carries a child in her womb; but her reprieve is for her child's sake, not her own. Likewise, had God slain wicked King Ahaz in his sin, good King Hezekiah would never have been born. God bore long with Israel's rebellion so that through them the Savior of sinners would be born. It is for His own name's sake He defers His anger. Like a patient captain, God waits until all His passengers are on board.

God's patience to the wicked is for the good of His people. Plucking up the tares now would damage the good plants. God would have spared Sodom for the sake of only a handful of God-fearing people. He also uses the wicked to perfect the patience of the saints. Whether by His patience to the wicked He protects us or proves us, it is for our advantage.

By God's patience, sinners are shown to be without excuse, and holy wrath is justified all the more. As wisdom is justified of its children, so justice is justified of the rebels against patience. How can men charge God with wronging them when it is they who have rejected His offers? Since God has the right to punish men after one sin, yet since He patiently bears with their many sins, how utterly inexcusable is man's continuance in sin? Thus, every sinner unquestionably deserves the wrath of God. God is longsuffering here that His justice may be more public hereafter.

Finally, the practical implications of this attribute must be applied to our hearts.

Instruction

God's patience is abused. Ultimately, every sinner is guilty of such abuse. Many a man misinterprets it and mistakes it for carelessness or neglect on God's part. Some even imagine it to be a consenting to their sins, making God an accomplice to their crimes. Because God in patience keeps silence, men think He is "altogether such a one as [themselves]" (Ps. 50:21). Any who continue in a course of sin abuse God's patience, as if God were protecting them so that they might rebel against Him. How many have discontinued sinning while under God's rod, but when He in patience removes the rod, they return to their former ways! They act as if God had restocked His patience so they might sin all the more. Thus, the patience that should melt them hardens them. Pharaoh was somewhat thawed under judgments but frozen again under God's forbearance. Men abuse this attribute by taking encouragement from it to descend to greater depths of sin. "Because sentence against an evil work is not executed speedily, therefore the heart of the sons of men is fully set in them to do evil" (Eccl. 8:11).

The abuse of this attribute is a great evil. Every new sin is committed against an increased degree of God's patience, rendering each successive sin more grievous and worthy of more punishment.

It is dangerous to abuse God's patience, for His patience will have an end. His "spirit shall not always strive with man" (Gen. 6:3). His patience ends at the end of a man's earthly lifetime. God has wrath to punish as well as patience to bear. Let none think that God has no anger simply because He is "slow to anger" (Pss. 103:8; 145:8; Joel 2:13, etc.). Though patience overrules justice by suspending it, justice will at last overrule patience by utterly silencing it. God is slow to pluck an arrow from His quiver and slow to place it in His bow, yet He hits the mark. How long He bore with the nation Israel but finally pulverized them to ashes by the power of the Romans! The more His patience is abused, the more awful will be the wrath He inflicts. While men are abusing this attribute, God is whetting His sword. The longer they sin, the sharper His edge is honed. The further He draws back in fetching His blow, the harder it will fall. When at last the time of judgment does come, it will be swift and severe. Then it shall be better to have suffered an earlier punishment than to have abused patience and store up a greater treasure of wrath. One of the great torments of hell will be to remember God's longsuffering and the inexcusable abuse of it.

This attribute explains why God lets His enemies oppress His people: only then could we see His power over Himself. He would not have gotten such a great name in delivering Israel in the days of Moses had He destroyed Pharaoh upon his first persecution against the nation.

This attribute explains why God lets sin remain in those who are regenerate: only thus could we ever personally know His patience. In heaven, there will be no place for this attribute, for there will be no provocation. This world is the only place for patience to appear. Hereafter it will remain closed up in the Deity.

Comfort

The patience of God carries a special meaning to believers. Our heavenly Father is a "God of patience and consolation" (Rom. 15:5). The first expression of comfort to Noah after his exit from the ark was the assurance of God's patience, that He would not destroy the earth any more with a flood (Gen. 9:11). Since the world did not improve any, it is evident that the manifestation of God's patience to the new world is greater than that manifested to the old world.

Why is God's patience comforting to believers?

❖ *Because it proves His grace to His people.* If He is patient toward those who will not repent and believe, how much more patient is He toward those who use His patience for its revealed purpose—to be led to repentance.

❖ *Because it provides a ground to trust in His promises.* If the provocations of men meet with an unwillingness on God's part to punish them, faith in Him will meet with the choicest embraces from Him.

❖ *Because it is a comfort in infirmities.* If God brought His saints to account for their every sin, what would become of us? We could not even complete a prayer! But God is a patient Father and spares us "as a man spareth his own son that serveth him" (Mal. 3:17). How He bears with our imperfect worship and service to Him!

Exhortation

Let us meditate often on the patience of God. How can we miss this attribute, when it is present in every bite of bread and every breath of air? Nothing pleases the devil more than to deface this attribute in our minds. But meditating on this excellent perfection in God will:

❖ *Make God lovelier to us.* In some respects, this attribute is more amazing than His goodness, which is toward all creation. Patience has to do with sinful creatures.

❖ *Make our repentance more frequent and more serious.* Realizing that we have sinned against such a gentle God as He should make us ashamed before Him. The fact that we still exist is not a testimony to the smallness of our sins but to the vastness of His patience. Oh, wretched man that I am, to abuse God's longsuffering so as to offend Him! Oh, infinite patience, to employ His power to preserve me that might have been used to punish me!

❖ *Make us resent more the injuries done by others to God.* Any patient sufferer attracts the pity of men. When we see God's patience slighted by men, it should make us take up God's cause.

❖ *Make us patient under the chastening hand of God.* If we knew how much He spares us, we would give thanks in our trials rather than repine.

Let us admire and be amazed at His patience and bless Him for it. Had we stolen from our neighbor, would he have withheld his vengeance, unless he had been too weak to carry it out? We have done worse to God, yet His sword remains in its scabbard. Surely in heaven, one great part of our anthems will be to praise God for the patience He showed toward us before He called us to Christ, in preserving our lives despite untold insults against Him. Only when, from a safe distance, we see our deserved hell will we recognize how much we owe to God. With Paul, let us see ourselves as the one to whom God showed forth all longsuffering (1 Tim. 1:16).

To elevate our thoughts concerning this attribute, let us mark:

❖ *The number of our sins.* Every moment we live is a moment of sin on our part and of patience on God's part. Think of the effect of but one sin upon Adam or Moses or Ananias and Sapphira. Thank God He has dealt patiently with us!

❖ *What low creatures we are.* Let us stand in awe of the God of glory who stoops down to wait on us worms of earth.

❖ *How high and holy is the One who waits on us.* One moment of patience from Him transcends all the patience of creatures of all time combined.

❖ *How long He has been patient thus far.* A man awaiting execution thinks it a privilege to have a reprieve for thirty days, but God has given to many a reprieve for thirty years or more, despite much greater offenses. The damned in hell would recognize it a great kindness to have but one day's respite as an opportunity in which to repent.

❖ *How much more patience God has shown to you than to others.* How many around you have been struck dead, yet you remain alive to this day! Were your crimes any less than theirs? Or is God simply more patient toward you? If

God had put an end to your earthly life before you had made provision for eternal life, how eternally deplorable would your condition have been! Let those whose past life was of a deeper dye consider this: God could have struck you dead while you were in the embrace of a harlot. And will you ever tire of praising Him for His exceeding great patience?

Let us not presume upon God's patience. Sinners must understand that though they are under God's patience, they are also under His wrath. "God is angry with the wicked every day" (Ps. 7:11). Do not continue to waste the precious opportunities God presently gives you that you might turn from your sin and turn to Him. Remember, hell is full of people who enjoyed the patience of God. Therefore, you must have more than His patience. His patience says that He is appeasable, but it does not say that He is appeased. An appeased God is the privilege only of those who genuinely repent of sin and savingly believe on the Lord Jesus Christ.

Let us imitate this attribute of God and be patient toward others. How unlike God is a man in a hurry! When God is patient toward our many injuries, how can we be hasty to get revenge on others for one small offense? It is in the context of doing good to our enemies that our Lord taught us to be like God. "Be ye therefore perfect, even as your Father which is in heaven is perfect" (Matt. 5:48). Let us therefore prove a power over our own spirits and be slow to anger.

Recent Titles from Free Grace Press

The Gospel Made Clear to Children
Jennifer Adams

Beautifully illustrated with short chapters, *The Gospel Made Clear to Children* details the person and work of Christ. It begins with the holiness of God, the sinfulness of man, and the penalty for sin. It considers the love of God in eternity past and the provision God has made in sending His Son. It traces the incarnation, birth, life, and ministry of Jesus Christ, with a special focus on His crucifixion, resurrection, ascension, and exaltation. It culminates with a call to repent and believe, ending with the evidence of true conversion. Written from a heart full of love, this book calls children to turn from their sins and trust in Christ.

The Gospel Made Clear to Children Study Guide
Jennifer Adams

The Gospel Made Clear to Children Study Guide is to be used alongside *The Gospel Made Clear to Children* book. This companion guide takes a deeper look into the Scripture verses mentioned in the book. The study questions promote reflection and application, moving truth from the head to the heart. The goal is to help children be not only hearers of the Word but also doers. Each section ends with a brief prayer, encouraging children to ask the Lord for grace and help.

"The highest recommendation I can give to this wonderful book is that I will be reading it over and over again to my children. It is rich in biblical doctrine and is an invaluable instrument to aid parents in teaching their children the glorious truths of "God in Christ" reconciling the world to Himself. I know of no other book that so clearly communicates the great doctrines of the gospel to children."

– Paul Washer,
Author, Director of HeartCry Missionary Society

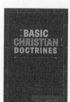

Basic Christian Doctrines
Dr. Curt Daniel

Basic Christian Doctrines is very much what the title suggests—a concise introduction to the fundamental doctrines taught in the Bible. In fifty short chapters consisting of ten simple points each, Daniel presents a thorough introduction to evangelical Christian theology. Those who want a short and non-technical summary of basic Christian theology will find this an excellent tool for Sunday school classes, home Bible studies, homeschools and Christian high schools, and personal Bible study. *Basic Christian Doctrines* is an important, useful handbook every Christian should keep close at hand.

> "Usually, other attempts to accomplish a work like this fall flat. Either the subjects are treated with far too much verbiage—thus unnecessarily lengthening the prose, or else easy enough to read but are much too elementary in content. Daniel, however, deftly succeeds with both aims where many other writers do not."
>
> – *Dr. Lance Quinn,*
> *Executive Vice-President, The Expositors Seminary, Jupiter, FL*

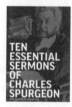

Ten Essential Sermons of Charles Spurgeon
Charles Spurgeon, with an introduction by Tom Nettles

> "Charles Haddon Spurgeon had no peer in the theological density of his sermons. At the same time, he had no peer in their simplicity. He looked at truth, to which Christ came to bear witness and embody, as the pathway not only for altering the mind but for shaping the affections. These ten sermons exemplify this pattern of deep doctrine, simple but elegant and engaging presentation, and a call to faith and love. ...The effort to isolate ten influential sermons from a preacher who preached thousands of such sermons is daunting. These sermons, however, succeed in illustrating Spurgeon's doctrine, his evangelistic commitment, the beauty of his language, the manner in which a biblical text suggests a subject, and his passion for the glory of the triune God and the eternal well-being of souls."
>
> – *from the introduction by Tom Nettles*

The Missionary Crisis: Five Dangers Plaguing Missions and How the Church Can Be the Solution
Paul Snider, foreword by Paul Washer

The Missionary Crisis confronts five dangers facing missionaries and the local churches that send them and gives biblical and practical instruction for missionaries, sending churches, and mission organizations. This book boldly approaches gentle correction for the missionary to reverse these five crises in their ministries. It challenges the local church to prepare and equip men and women for the high calling of missionary life.

"Paul Snider's book, *The Missionary Crisis*, is like looking through a window. He divulges the plight of modern missions with engaging reality. As a missionary, Paul's perspective will afford the reader a much greater concern for what is called today kingdom advancement. Years ago, a mission director said that "the mission field is littered with uncrucified flesh." His assessment, both then and now, is accurate. But Paul doesn't stop after exposing the encumbrances to global missions; he offers biblical and practical solutions to the problems. Local churches, mission agencies, and anyone with an interest in gospel mission enterprise will profit immensely from this superb work."

– Don Currin, HeartCry Missionary Society
Eastern European Coordinator

Biblical Foundations of Corporate Worship
Scott Aniol

Ever since Cain and Abel, God's people have been asking, "What is the proper way to worship God?" In five compelling chapters, Scott Aniol explains that corporate worship theology and practice must be founded in the Word of God. There, we discover that corporate worship's goal is communion with God through regular, weekly covenant renewal, wherein the entire congregation engages in dialogue with God in a meeting structured around the gospel, toward the goal of spiritual fellowship with God through Christ by the Spirit.

"The devilish attack of deformation transcends beyond the doctrines of Scripture to the functionality of the church. The church and Scripture are inextricably bound together. Therefore, the need of the hour is biblical reformation of the church's worship. Scott Aniol does an excellent job of directing our attention to Scripture and warning us of the steady stream of man-centered worship philosophies that are constantly luring Christians outside the boundaries of Scripture."

—*Josh Buice, Pastor, Pray's Mill Baptist Church, Douglasville, GA,*
President, G3 Ministries

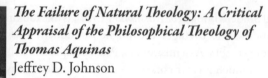

The Failure of Natural Theology: A Critical Appraisal of the Philosophical Theology of Thomas Aquinas
Jeffrey D. Johnson

"Johnson's scholarly but gracefully readable text shows that his intellect notwithstanding, Aquinas's mingled metaphysics, mixed methodology, and promotion of "divine immobility" merit strong caution. This is the book the church has needed on this subject. It is an urgent read by one of our best theologians."

—*Dr. Owen Strachan*

"Jeff's book is a welcome contribution to the debate that is and should be going on in Reformed circles about the value of Thomism in general and the usefulness of his natural theology in particular."

—*Dr. Sam Waldron*

Seven Thoughts Every Christian Ought to Think Every Day: Laying a Foundation for a Life of Prayer
Jim Scott Orrick

In *Seven Thoughts Every Christian Ought to Think Every Day*, Jim Scott Orrick examines the seven thoughts that lead Christians to pray guided by the model prayer. You might think of this book as a prequel to the Lord's Prayer. Without the underlying thoughts of a renewed nature, simply repeating the Lord's Prayer becomes an instance of the empty, meaningless prayers that Jesus was teaching us to avoid. Orrick explores the seven thoughts that propel a Christian into a life of meaningful communion with God through prayer. These are seven thoughts every Christian ought to think every day, and they lay a foundation for a life of prayer.

"Searching for great resources to disciple new believers can be like Goldilocks tasting porridge. Too difficult, and it frustrates; too fluffy, and it misleads. Jim Orrick has that much sought-after gift of taking deep truths and bringing the tray to the common man. When a book can be handed to an unbeliever for evangelism, read through with a new believer to disciple, worked through with the family for worship, and also delight the soul of the seasoned in Christ, it is a helpful book."

– *Josh Lagrange, Church planter*

On Your Heart: A Three-Year Devotional for Families
A.J. Genco

In 2003, inspired by USAF Colonel Rick Husband of the space shuttle Columbia, A. J. Genco set out to write a devotional for his own family, laboring over it for ten years. Yet when he had barely finished, he was taken from this earth by a sudden illness. Though this devotional was never intended for publication, A. J.'s widow desired for it to be published to honor his legacy. Now not only may you and your family be blessed by this resource but we also hope you would be inspired to leave a spiritual legacy for your own family.

This book includes:

- A family devotional based on a three-year cycle through the Bible
- A "Read through the Bible" guide for parents and older children
- Daily "Family Worship" lessons for the whole family
- A psalm or a portion of a psalm to read each Sunday
- Excerpts from the Baptist Confession of Faith and Nicene Creed

Baptist Reprints Series

Christ Precious to Those Who Believe
John Fawectt

Written in 1799, *Christ Precious to Those Who Believe* by John Fawcett is a "minor spiritual classic of the eighteenth century that deserves to be better known. In it, Fawcett explores the way that 'love is the parent and promoter of everything excellent and amiable in the Christian character,' a love that is, first and foremost, a love for the Lord Jesus Christ" (adapted from the introductio by Michael Haykin).

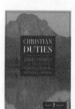

Christian Duties
Zenas Trivett

Christian Duties, originally entitled *Plain Christian Duties Recommended*, is an address Zenas Trivett gave at the establishment of a new Baptist congregation in 1791, in which he lays out the various responsibilities of a faithful member of a local church. Trivett emphasized that congregational polity was "the alone [only] plan of the New Testament," though he urged his hearers never to dream that "all true religion [is] confined to your own denomination." He particularly urged the congregation to often "meet together . . . for prayer and conversation," for believers who come together "destitute of the spirit of devotion," Trivett noted, have "their cold affections warmed.".

A Choice Drop of Honey from the Rock of Christ
Thomas Wilcox

Thomas Wilcox wrote this little book before the Great Fire of London in 1666—A *Choice Drop of Honey from the Rock Christ*. This book has gone through many editions and translations. Though a small book, it has been greatly used by God throughout the centuries. And though it has often been reprinted, it has fallen out of print in our day. Thus, it is our pleasure to bring this treasure back into circulation..

Baptists: Thorough Reformers
John Quincy Adams

What does it mean to be a Baptist? Though ideas abound, we must go to the one man for a sure answer, John Quincy Adams. For with unashamed boldness and clarity, Adams articulates the fundamental distinctives of the Baptist faith. These fundamentals include the importance of sola Scriptura, believer's baptism, the separation of the church and state, equality of the saints, and liberty of conscience. Even C. H. Spurgeon, calling it "the best Manual of Baptist principles he had met," included the text in his Pastor's College curriculum. First published in 1858 and reprinted multiple times since, this work has become a classic tome on Baptist principles. And 150 years later, we too, affirming the testimony of Spurgeon and countless others, are happy to release this updated edition of *Baptists: The Only Thorough Religious Reformers* as the first volume in our Baptist Reprints series.

The Glory of a True Church
Benjamin Keach

"Because of their historical context at the beginning of the Baptist movement, the seventeenth-century English Baptists thought deeply about the nature of the church. Their writings are an important corrective to the lackadaisical approach taken by many in our day. Benjamin Keach's The Glory of a True Church is the climax of the seventeenth-century Baptist literature on the church. It remains a faithful guide for pastors and churches to aid them in a recovering of a biblical understanding of the church."

—G. Stephen Weaver, Jr., PhD,
Senior Pastor, Farmdale Baptist Church

**Visit
www.FreeGracePress.com
for these and many
other excellent resources.**